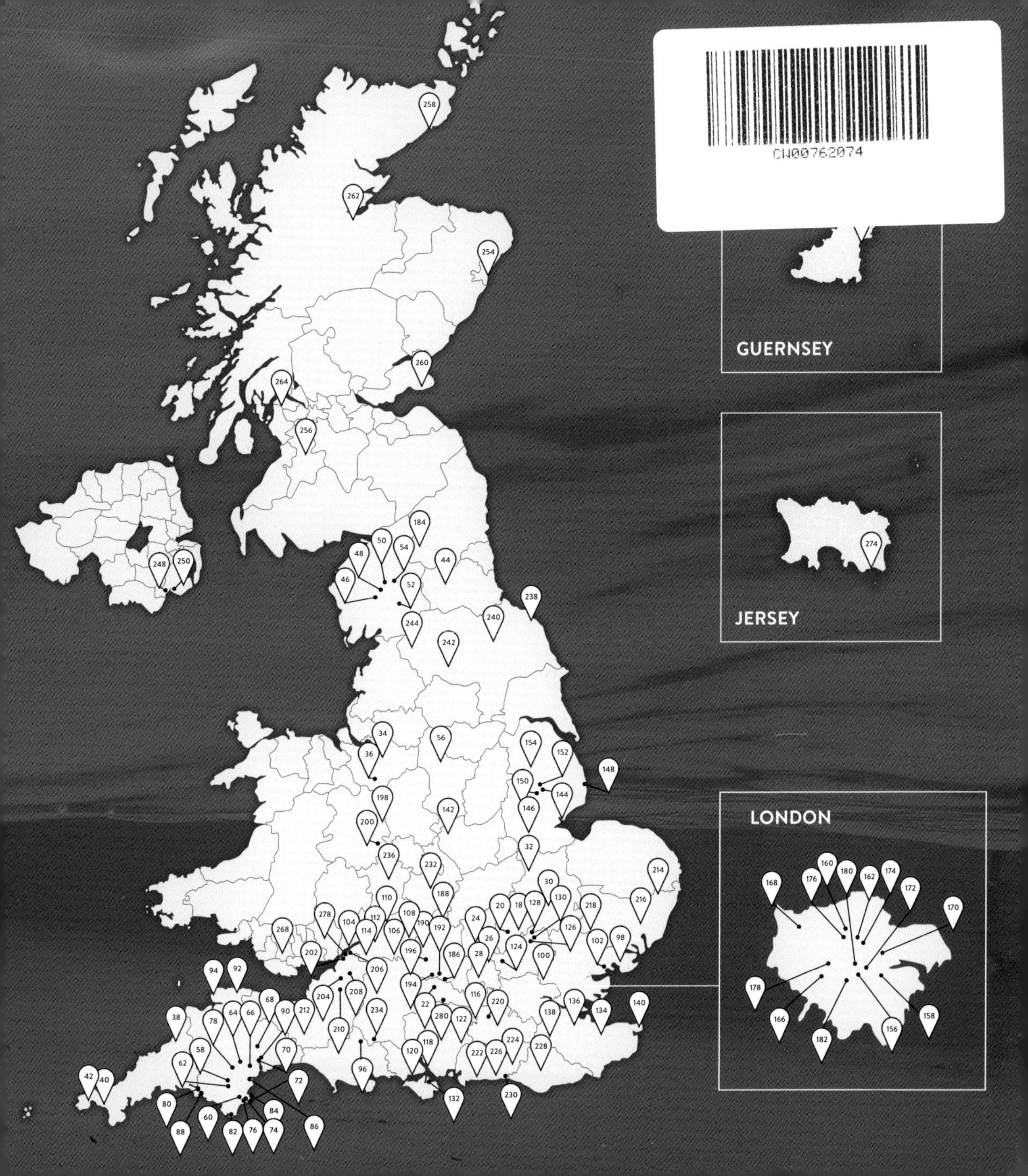
GUERNSEY
JERSEY
LONDON

THE LIDO GUIDE

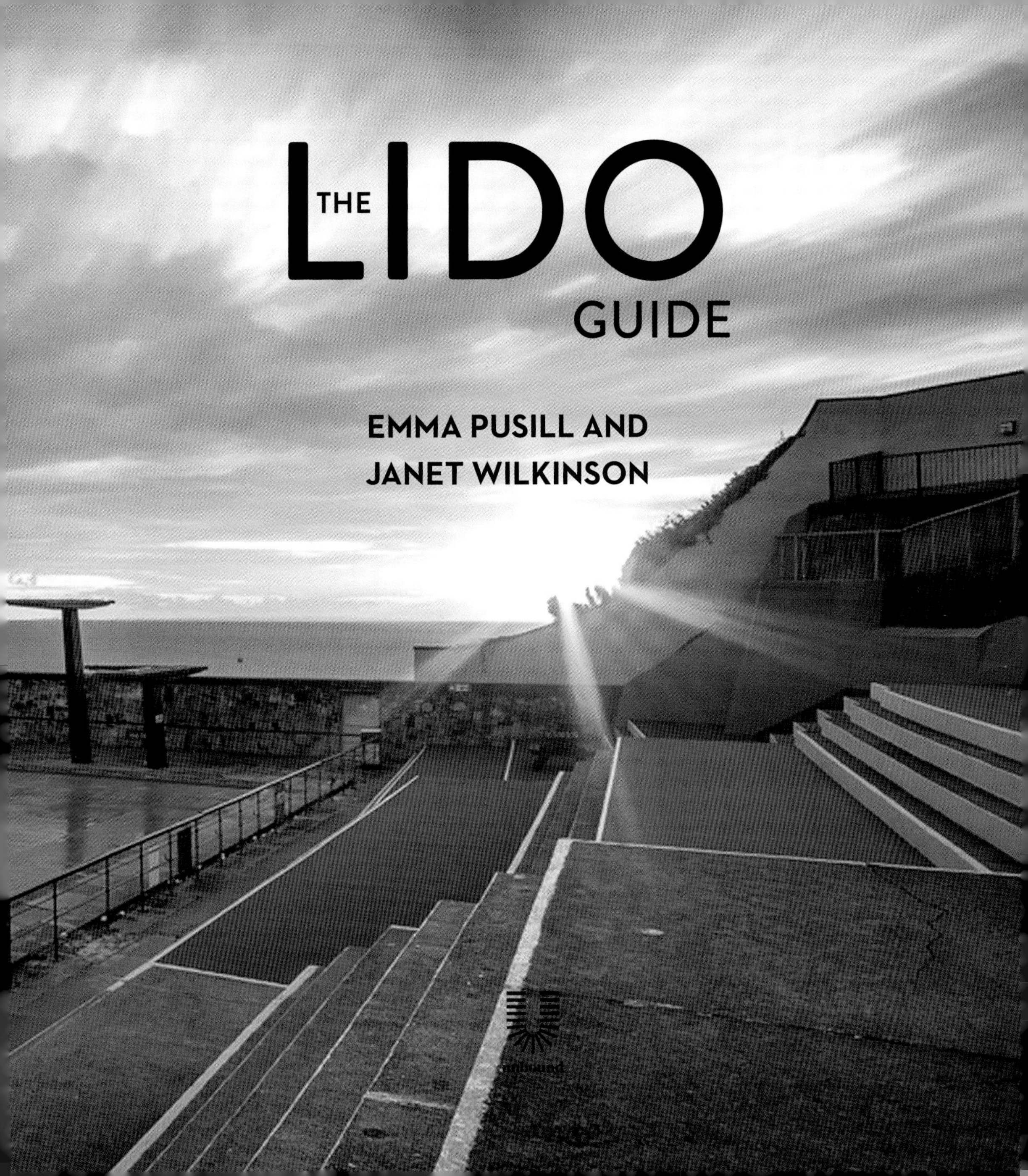
THE LIDO GUIDE
EMMA PUSILL AND
JANET WILKINSON
unbound

This edition first published in 2019
Unbound
6th Floor Mutual House, 70 Conduit Street, London W1S 2GF
www.unbound.com

Text design by carrdesignstudio.com

A CIP record for this book is available from the British Library

ISBN 978-1-78352-742-7 (trade pbk)
ISBN 978-1-78352-744-1 (ebook)

Printed in China by 1010 Printing International Limited

Previous page: *Portishead Open Air Pool, Somerset* © Ben Maliphant

Opposite: *Parliament Hill Lido, London* © Roger Taylor

Following page: *The Strand Leisure Pool, Kent*

For Sophie, Izaak and all generations of lido lovers

Inspiration

Ashley Norris for his *Guardian* article in July 2002 where he swam in eight London lidos in a day – a pioneer of the lido road trip.

Oliver Merrington and Andy Hoines for their early webpages telling us where we could find lidos across the UK. Janet plotted these on a map way back in 2004, and that map formed the backbone of her early lido journey.

Janet Smith for her book *Liquid Assets* in 2005; we love all of it, but particularly the list of lidos at the back.

Kate Rew for her book *Wild Swim* and its coverage of lidos.

Roger Deakin for the ideas and stories in *Waterlog: A Swimmer's Journey Through Britain*.

We've not met any of you and yet you have inspired us to swim, travel, tweet and write.

This book has been a long time in the making.

Because we could

RECOMMENDED

CONTENTS

THE LIDOS

England

Northern Ireland

Scotland

Wales

Channel Islands

You Say Lee-doh, We Say Ly-doh

Opposite: *Beccles Lido, Suffolk*

INTRODUCTION

Lidos change lives, we have no doubts about this. One of the ways they do this is by drawing people together. We were drawn together by our shared interest in open-air pools, first meeting online via Twitter. It didn't take us many conversations to realise that we had noticed very similar things about the pools we had visited. Some of them were hard to find, we rarely had any idea what to expect when we got there, and opening hours were something of a lucky dip. Making any kind of contact with some pools was also a challenge. We assumed it required some sort of coded smoke signals, or swimming-towel semaphore. At least we assumed that, because calling or emailing ahead didn't always tell us what we wanted to know, even if we managed to get an answer.

During one of our many conversations about the practicalities of visiting one pool or another the idea for *The Lido Guide* evolved. A book like this would have made our lido road trips so much easier to plan and enjoy. We knew we needed it, and we were convinced other people would need it too. But, more than that, we thought that the pools themselves needed this book; just as swimmers need pools, pools need swimmers. One cannot be without the other.

Most of the remaining lidos in the UK are now community run by an army of volunteers – people who have stepped up to save pools that local authorities no longer have any interest in running. These pools are the backbone of the lido scene in the UK. They are as diverse and individual as the communities that cherish them.

Opposite: *Lymington Sea Water Baths, Hampshire*

Below: *Brightlingsea Open Air Swimming Pool, Essex*

While no two are alike, many of them have one thing in common. They operate on a financial knife-edge. You'll see them working hard to raise funds to survive and thrive, and while they will always welcome donations, what is most valuable to them is income – in other words, your admission money, your cake money, the cash you part with for that lovely swimming towel, cap or kit bag with a picture of the pool printed on it.

In writing this book, we are motivated by a desire to see the number of swimmers using these pools increase, because that will help to secure their futures. It is, after all, a great deal for swimmers. When you make a donation to a pool, you get a warm glow of pleasure. When you pay to actually swim there you get that warm glow PLUS a swim, a bit of lido chat with the staff, volunteers and regulars, and in all likelihood a cuppa and a slice of cake afterwards. The pool gets income, satisfaction from seeing swimmers enjoy the fruits of their labours and, hopefully, some excellent publicity when you spread the word about your marvellous swim.

We also hope to inspire you to use these pools on the wet, grey days as well as the blisteringly blue ones. You'll see plenty of photographs in this book with leaden skies over the blue of the water. The income level of most outdoor pools can be directly tied to how good a summer the UK has experienced: there are a lot of fair-weather lido lovers out there. If you've bought this book there is every chance that you're not one of them. You already know the pleasures of swimming in warm water while rain prickles your shoulders, and wind licks over your wet arms. You probably know how exalted you feel when you break the water diving into an empty pool; it's a feeling you'll never experience if you only use lidos when the sun is out and they are thronged with fair-weather swimmers. If you don't already know these pleasures, we urge you to taste them for yourselves. Shed the fair-weather-lido-lover mantle and embrace the worst the British weather can throw at you.

Left: *Parliament Hill Lido, London* © Annabel Lavers

Above: *Pells Pool, Sussex*

Once you have come to love swimming in the rain and gales, you might be tempted to complain about the crowds on hot days, when you are so used to having free run of 'your' pool. We are NEVER cross about having to queue to visit a lido when the sun is out. We look at every swimmer standing in line ahead of us and see the colour of their money. It is busy-day income that keeps pools open on wet Tuesday afternoons in June. It is busy-day income that pays for you to have the thrill of diving into that empty pool, that funds every swim you've ever ended by floating on your back, looking at the sky and revelling in being alone with your thoughts and the water. Be happy about those queues. Embrace them. Welcome what they do for the future of a pool.

But before you can even think about joining a lido queue, you need to know where you are going. Not all lidos or open-air pools in the UK are in the most obvious of places. Sometimes you think, 'Can it really be down here? Is this it?' The answers are, yes, it often can be down there, and yes, this could be it! For all the glamour of the regularly featured or written about open-air pools in the UK, there are a host of pools that are smaller, run in small communities, often rural, and where you need to plan your route and arrival in advance. We've provided as much detail as possible here in the guide, but it is still worth checking everything ahead of time.

We've both parked in some interesting places over the years to go in search of an outdoor swim, because it wasn't easy to discover, before we set out, what the parking arrangements would be at the pool. Or we've gone by train and had some fascinating walks when the station hasn't been quite as close to the pool as it appeared on the maps we had; especially prior to Google Maps!

When you've made it as far as the front door you'll be raring to go, cossie and goggles in hand. It's time to hand over your money and rush on in. And in some pools you might, literally, have to do just that, as they haven't yet embraced the credit-card economy. Always travel with some cash in your swim bag if you don't want to have the difficult job of explaining to any younger swimmers in the party that you won't, after a two-hour drive to the pool, be swimming after all. We don't quote the admission charges in each pool's entry, because that is subject to change and varies depending on your age, the size of your party and how long you want to stay. Instead, we give you all the information you need to contact a pool and find out the current position. Some pools offer season tickets, multi-swim tickets or a monthly membership-type subscription. These can be excellent value if you're lucky enough to live or work locally. In the main, you can expect to pay between £5 and £10 for an adult casual swim. Some pools are a little cheaper, and a few are considerably more expensive.

Once you've navigated the admissions desk, hopefully having had a lovely chat with a volunteer on the way in, you need to be prepared for a wide variety of changing facilities. Some are very basic, and some are very swish. Many, but not all, lidos will have lockers on offer, so keep a handful of small change in your bag. It's also a good idea to ask at the desk if the lockers take tokens, and if so, which kind. They aren't standard, and checking up front avoids the walk of shame back to the desk in your cossie when you discover that none of your vast collection of tokens fit. So few pools have no lockers at all that we haven't specified that in the entries, but whether there are lockers or not, it is probably wise not to take anything of enormous value with you.

So now you're changed, you're poolside and you're ready to get wet. It may seem obvious, but we'll say it anyway: you need to be prepared for the possibility that you might not get the kind of swim you were expecting or hoping for. Most, but not all, of the pools in this book have a varied timetable of sessions catering to all types of swimmer, so if ploughing up and down the pool for a refreshing workout swim is your intention, then focus on lane sessions or wet afternoons when a lido will

Left: *Tunnels Beaches, Devon*

Right: *Faversham Outdoor Pool, Kent*

Above: *Lazonby Pool, Cumbria* © Jill Eastham

typically be quiet. If it's a hot day when all and sundry have come for the opportunity to cool off and alternate taking the occasional dip with time spent relaxing on the side, then you can expect a lido to have removed any lanes to maximise capacity. Many of the pools in this book lend themselves to a day trip, and you can while away the hours. But some of them run time-limited sessions, so checking the website is important. Where there is plenty of space around the pool for loafing about, we've mentioned it to help you if you are visiting with the intention of spending all afternoon/day there.

Many swimmers will want a little memento of a visit to a lido, and there is an opportunity for a little retail therapy at an increasing number of pools, where you can buy mugs, key rings, cotton bags, swimming hats, postcards and a good deal else besides to remind you of your visit. This all helps to generate income to keep the pool going, and provides you with a souvenir of your visit that is worth taking a little extra cash along for.

Of course, the most popular way to create a memento is to take photos. All pools have different policies on this. Some pools are very relaxed about it, but you might not be allowed to take photos at others, or you might have to complete a permission form. Approaches to this vary widely and, consequently, so might your photo opportunities. As we travelled around the pools taking photographs for this book, we sometimes found it difficult to secure permission or agreements. As a result, some of the images in this book don't show off the pools to their best advantage. The most important thing to do is ask the staff or volunteers if the signage isn't clear. Some pools have signs up saying 'no photography', but if you ask permission then you may well be allowed to take a photograph or two to remember your trip by. If you are allowed to take photographs, we also advocate having a good look at what's going on in the background before you share them on social media. It might be a great selfie of you, but spare a thought for the person behind you struggling to get changed under a wind-whipped, slightly-too-small towel: they might be less enthusiastic about you sharing that picture of them with your thousands of Instagram followers.

After your swim it's quite likely that you will, if you are anything like us, be hungry. We are both keen swimmers who love to be actually *in the pool,* but in recent years the post-swim tea, cake and chat have become almost as important a part of the visit! This is true for others too. The equally itinerant @FancyaCuppaNow on Twitter is another outdoor-swimming fan who writes about the cups of tea and coffee enjoyed *after* the swims. This confirms we're not the only people who understand how well swimming and snacks go together. To that end we've made sure every entry in this guide gives you some information about what type of catering you can expect to find at each pool featured.

By now you'll be realising that what this book aims to do is signpost you to all the information you need to make a success of your lido visit, and to share a little of our adventures as we've swum our way around them. We hope that our experiences, coupled with the images in this book, paint a picture that has you reaching for your togs and packing your swim bag. Every trip to a lido, every experience, will be different, but the more excursions we can inspire, the better!

We end this introduction with a disclaimer of sorts. Pools change. Sometimes very quickly. In the six months we spent writing and editing the first draft of this manuscript, a number of pools altered their operating models, their social media details and their opening hours. We have done everything in our power to make this book as up to date as possible when going to print, but there is always the possibility that by the time you hold it in your hands some things may have changed. Please let us know about it if you find an inaccuracy.

And please let us know about your lido road trips. We love to hear about them, and so do the pools. Your enthusiasm, shared via social media, is the best publicity they can get. Send them a tweet, tag them in your Instagram posts, leave a review or comment on their Facebook page or TripAdvisor. You'll be rewarding the hard work that goes into preserving these pools in a tangible, practical and useful way. And maybe, just maybe, by spreading the lido love you'll inspire others to enjoy these places as well.

You can tell us about your lido road trips on Facebook, Twitter and Instagram, where our user name is @LidoGuide. Use #LidoRoadTrip and we're sure to see it.

Emma and Janet

LIDO LANGUAGE AND A GUIDE TO THE PRACTICAL STUFF

You say Lee-doh, I say Ly-doh

In the open-air swimming community many debates abound. The top three we end up engaging in are: *What exactly constitutes a lido? Are all open-air pools lidos? How do you pronounce the word lido?*

This book has been crowdfunded by lots of different people, so it seems appropriate to use the crowdsourced definition of lido from Wikipedia.

> A lido (/ˈliːdoʊ/ LEE-doh, /ˈlaɪdoʊ/ LY-doh) is a public outdoor swimming pool and surrounding facilities, or part of a beach where people can swim, lie in the sun, or participate in water sports. On a cruise ship or ocean liner, the lido deck features outdoor pools and related facilities.
>
> *Lido* is an Italian word for 'beach' and forms part of the place name of several Italian seaside towns known for their beach, e.g., Lido di Venezia, the barrier beach enclosing the Venetian Lagoon. Possibly the term found its way into English from English visitors returning from the Lido di Venezia, where sea-bathing took place from the late nineteenth century.

As swimmers and writers we use the term lido and outdoor pool interchangeably, *but* a specific pool you visit might not refer to itself as a lido. Some, for example, favour 'open-air pool' or 'baths'.

And the pronunciation – is it lee-doh or ly-doh? It is both. It is whatever is most comfortable for you to think, say and enjoy. Keeping with the Italian connection, there's a saying that suggests:

> In Italy my dog is called Guido and I say Lee-doh.
>
> In the UK my dog is called Fido and I say Ly-doh.

We're really clear about what we mean when we say lido and in our view, if you have a different definition or pronunciation, that is completely fine with us; it means you are in the conversation.

Left: *Gourock Pool, Renfrewshire*

Criteria for inclusion

For the purposes of this book we've defined the criteria for being a *publicly accessible lido* as:

- you can turn up and pay for swim there without having to be a member
- you can swim in the pool, i.e. it is not a paddling pool
- there are some man-made features of the pool (e.g. sides, ladders, changing rooms/areas) designating this as a public swimming space.

You'll see this definition has been stretched to its limits in parts, but we have been clear in the text when we've done that.

Above: *Ilkley Lido, Yorkshire* © Richard Haines

Below: *Park Road Pools and Fitness, London*

Geography

We've tried to make *The Lido Guide* easy to use, with pools listed under both the country and county in which they sit. As you plan your travels about the UK we hope this will make it easy to find the pool, or pools, closest to your destination. It should also make it straightforward to discover pools that would make a useful break in a longer journey; some are very easily accessible from motorways and main roads, and where that is the case we've mentioned it in the pool's entry. Once you've broken a journey with a swim at a lido you'll loathe using service stations ever again. (Or, as the case is most likely to be, loathe using service stations even more than you already do.)

Operating models 

You'll notice that we discuss the operating models and refreshments for each pool. We've used some standardised terminology throughout:

- **Privately run** – a facility owned by the operator, and run on a for-profit basis.
- **Volunteer run** – a facility primarily run by volunteers, although the structure of that may vary; some staff, most often lifeguards, will be paid but you can expect many of the people you see in other roles at the pool to be volunteers.
- **Corporately run on behalf of the council** – a facility that has been put out to tender by the local authority, and is run under contract. The organisations running these pools are often registered charities, but the pool is run in a corporate way, in that all staff will be paid, there may be an enhanced focus on the bottom line and if the organisation runs other facilities you will notice a recognisable brand style at each location.
- **Charitable-trust run** – the trustees may well be volunteers, but they primarily rely on paid staff to run the facility on the ground.
- **Council run** – a facility that is owned by a local authority who does not put the operation of the pool out to contract, but manages it in-house and employs its own staff to run it.

Sometimes two of these operating models combine effectively, such as at Stonehaven, where there is a very healthy partnership between the local authority and the volunteers, and where that is the case we mention it.

Above: *Stonehaven Open Air Swimming Pool, Aberdeenshire*

Refreshments 

Likewise, with food and drink, we've standardised the terms we use into the following categories:

- **Snack kiosk** – the pool serves food that you eat outside, around the pool. The offering at kiosks varies wildly, everything from a fridge freezer full of lollies in the staff room to quite sophisticated menus with hot and cold food. They key point, however, is that there is no indoor seating attached to a kiosk.
- **On-site café** – food will be served where there is an indoor seating area with tables and chairs; again, the standard of the offering can vary widely. From the well-respected café at Brockwell Lido, which is so popular that booking ahead is advisable, to the rather less sought after cafés of the sort we are familiar with at leisure centres.
- **None available** – this is as you expect, but where there are options nearby we have tried to mention them.
- **Picnics** – we have not explicitly stated which pools welcome picnics, as with the exception of Thames Lido and Bristol Lido the overwhelming majority of pools are very happy for you to take your own food, but please leave glass and ceramics at home.

Left above: *Bathurst Open Air Pool, Gloucestershire*

Left below: *Ashburton Swimming Pool, Devon*

Accessibility

In respect of disability access it is fair to say that many lidos recognise a need to do more, having been somewhat hampered by elderly infrastructure and limited funds. This is changing, and it will continue to change. We have made every effort to give accurate and helpful information, but if you have a particular need or query we strongly recommend that you phone the pool ahead of your visit as the situation can be very changeable.

Below: *Faversham Outdoor Pool, Kent*

Key to symbols

Monday 12/03 ✓

Tick and date your first swim in each lido here

- Email address
- Telephone
- Website
- Twitter
- Facebook
- Instagram
- Tank size
- Operating model
- Opening times
- Water temperature
- Water type
- Parking
- Refreshments

AN HISTORIC PERSPECTIVE

Historic Pools of Britain was established in 2015 to represent the nation's indoor and outdoor historic pools. With so many architectural and community gems lost, it was recognised that by giving one voice to all, the future of each might be made more secure.

Below: *Cleveland Pools, Somerset* © Tony McNicol Photography

The term 'historic' generally refers to pre-1945 pools, though there are a number of notable post-war pools that are deemed historic, including some that are formally listed by Historic England as being of architectural or historic significance. Historic Pools of Britain champions all these wonderful pools; it seeks to raise awareness of the significant contribution they make to the

HISTORIC POOLS OF BRITAIN

✉ info@historicpools.org.uk
☎ 0161 832 3588
historicpools.org.uk

social, sporting and architectural history of Great Britain and the fact that they continue to play an important role in our communities today.

Historic pools have seen hard times and many have been lost or are now threatened. At the same time, there are many examples of historic pools being saved and thriving. Many lidos, and an increasing number of indoor pools, have been rescued by local residents, with inspiring community campaigns active across the country. Other historic pools are run successfully by not-for-profit leisure trusts or public bodies and a few by enterprising private owners.

Historic Pools of Britain was set up as a membership organisation so that it could bring together all those bodies and individuals involved in the protection, restoration and operation of heritage pools. Members gain a lot by meeting up, visiting other historic pools and sharing their experiences. Events are held twice a year, always at a pool, and these are open to both members and non-members.

As well as mutual support and shared learning, a collective voice is provided for members through the media and public affairs. Gill Wright, who works for one of the organisation's founding members, Victoria Baths, acts as spokesperson and the management and communications is carried out by specialist consultants Fido PR. As a result Historic Pools has been making quite a splash across a range of media including BBC Radio 4's Today programme, the *Guardian*, *The Times*, the *Telelgraph*, the *Mirror*, plus magazines, online outlets and radio networks.

The Lido Guide is about celebrating, discovering and enjoying this unique part of our sporting and cultural heritage, making it a natural partner for Historic Pools of Britain, which is proud to be supporting the publication. While not all the pools are historic, they are all special, and we know that users of *The Lido Guide* will gain a great deal of enjoyment from the experience that awaits them.

To find out more about Historic Pools of Britain, visit the website, which will introduce you to members, highlight the national picture of historic pools and share the latest news. New members and enquiries about membership are very welcome.

THE LIDOS
ENGLAND

Marbury Park Open Air Pool, Cheshire

EVERSHOLT SWIMMING POOL

ENGLAND Bedfordshire

Eversholt Swimming Pool
Recreation Ground, Tyrells End, Eversholt,
Milton Keynes
Bedfordshire
MK17 9DS

- eversholtswimmingpool@gmail.com
- 01525 280515
- eversholtswimmingpool.co.uk
- @eversholtpool
- @eversholtpool

- 20 m x 7 m
- Volunteer run
- Seasonal
- Heated
- Freshwater
- Parking available on site
- Snack kiosk

The village of Eversholt is at the heart of the small county of Bedfordshire, and Eversholt Swimming Pool is at the heart of the village. On the wall of the village hall, adjacent to the pool, is a mosaic map of the village constructed in 2000 as part of Eversholt's celebration of the millennium. It shows the pool in a small number of bright blue tile pieces, next to the village hall and overlooking the cricket pitch and parish church.

And in reality it is just like that. This is one of the most picturesque settings for an outdoor swimming pool in this guide (and we don't say that lightly!). A 20-metre heated pool

built adjacent to the village hall, this lido is sheltered by a high stone wall on one side and looks directly out over the cricket pitch and onwards towards the church through a series of large glass windows down the other side of the pool.

The pool itself is not big but is great for laps on a quiet day. It's best to ring ahead and make sure the pool is going to be open as it relies upon volunteers to run it and Eversholt is not a natural tourist destination, hidden away from main roads, although close to the M1 and a few miles from Woburn Lido. It is good for a family visit too, with a semicircular shallow end for very little ones and plenty of room alongside the pool to sit and dry off. The big separate male and female communal changing rooms make getting a family changed and ready easy, and while there is no dedicated disabled changing area, the pool advises us that the accessible toilet can be used for that purpose. They don't have a hoist, but are happy to discuss any swimmer's specific needs in advance if you call them. As an example, they have a staff member who signs, and have been able to support group swims for hearing-impaired children by varying the way the lifeguards work. The sale of sweets and ice creams at reception completes the treat of a swim here.

Car parking is free in the village and close to the swimming pool, and this would make a good lido road trip with a visit to nearby Woburn.

WOBURN LIDO

ENGLAND Bedfordshire

Woburn Lido
Crawley Road, Woburn
Bedfordshire
MK17 9QG

- woburnlido@outlook.com
- 01525 290611
- woburn-lido.moonfruit.com
- @Woburnlido
- @woburnlido

- 22 m x 8 m
- Independent trust
- Seasonal
- Heated
- Freshwater
- Parking at the village hall opposite the lido (MK17 9QD)
- Snack kiosk

This 22-metre by 8-metre heated pool is on the edge of the beautiful village and estate of Woburn, not far from the outdoor pool in Eversholt. It has lots of free parking – some directly outside the pool and some across the road.

This is a community pool in every sense of the word and is over a hundred years old. Like so many of the pools featured in this guide, it has survived for so long thanks to the efforts of the community it sits in. The pool is run by volunteers, and as a visitor to the community you'll find the lido a welcoming place to be.

A pleasant walk from the centre of Woburn, with car parking outside and across the road, this is a sunny rural spot to swim on a warm day. There is plenty of space and some tables and chairs to sit at while you enjoy an ice cream from the snack kiosk. Picnics are welcome here, and

there are plenty of grassy spots to spread out your blanket.

The changing rooms here are in a new block (rather unusually but very effectively constructed as a triangular building!) and include a disabled-accessible changing area, some small cubicles and showers as well as the snack kiosk and lifeguard station. There is level or ramped access around the site.

NORTHCROFT LIDO

ENGLAND Berkshire

Northcroft Lido
Northcroft Leisure Centre, Northcroft Lane,
Newbury
Berkshire
RG14 1RS

- northcroft@parkwood-leisure.co.uk
- 01635 311999
- leisurecentre.com/northcroft-leisure-centre
- @NorthcroftLC

- 72 m x 10 m
- Corporately run on behalf of the council
- Seasonal
- Heated
- Freshwater
- Parking available on site
- On-site café

It is no understatement to say that the outdoor swimming experience at Northcroft Leisure Centre in Newbury is a complete surprise. The approach from the car park outside has you wondering whether you have come to the right place. This is a bustling and large leisure centre with a sports hall, gym, squash courts, classes and a 25-metre indoor pool; so far, so standard.

Then you follow the signs to the seasonal outdoor pool, and, like entry via the Narnia wardrobe, you find yourself on the other side of the very standard leisure centre changing rooms in another world. There is a long, narrow blue lido dominating a grassy, green site with the distinctive yellow accents of the pool entry steps, lifeguard stations and information signs.

This is another of those lidos where you pretty much can't wait

to get in, stuffing your clothes as quickly as possible into a poolside locker. The shallow end is unusually shallow (so, no tumble turns!) but there is a separate, decent-sized toddler pool next to the main pool that attracts the little ones.

The 72-metre swimming pool is a great place for methodically ploughing up and down, losing yourself in the cool blue depths.

The pool is heated just enough to take the edge off entry into the water, rather than to make it a toasty swimming experience, and the opportunity to swim long lengths looking upwards at the surrounding trees and rooftops, or by focusing your gaze and exhalations downwards towards the blue-painted tank, is a treat that few modern pools can offer.

There's a café on site but the pool is also within walking distance of Newbury town centre where there are plenty of other opportunities for food and drink. It would be easy to overlook Newbury as a place that hosts this treat of a lido – chances are that most of us pass this town at speed on the M4 or the A34 and don't think, *Oooh, I wonder if there's an open-air pool anywhere near here?* However, there's a rather nice potential lido road trip along both of these major highways; Newbury would make a great addition to a trip swimming in Abingdon, Hinksey and Woodstock pools to the north along the A34, or Lymington or Hilsea if you were heading south on the A34. If you're travelling along the M4 it also connects nicely with Bristol Lido and Thames Lido, and is within striking distance of Gulidford Lido.

There is level access throughout the site, and there are disabled-accessible changing facilities. The tank, however, is accessed by ladders and there is no hoist.

AQUA VALE POOL

ENGLAND Buckinghamshire

Aqua Vale Pool
Park Street, Aylesbury
Buckinghamshire
HP20 1DX

aquavaleinfo@everyoneactive.com
01296 488555
everyoneactive.com/aquavale
@eaAquaVale
@eaAquaVale

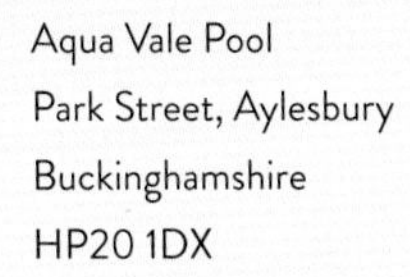

20 m x 10 m
Corporately run on behalf of the council
Year round
Heated
Freshwater
Parking available on site
On-site café

Aqua Vale Pool in Aylesbury has a 20-metre outdoor element within the centre, which also offers a 25-metre pool, fun pool and lazy river. However, the outdoor element of the pool complex has been roofed over with a retractable sliding roof and its opening depends very much on the weather, so it may only be an open-air pool on particularly warm and sunny days. We'd definitely recommend ringing ahead to see whether the pool will be open air on a day you plan to visit, and also suggest that there might be long queues to get in on those days!

The centre has the standard changing village approach to cubicles and lockers that many larger leisure centres have, and with a café on site there is everything you could want from an outdoor swim – as long as the retractable roof is open!

You'll find the pool in the town centre of Aylesbury, so it's accessible by train or car, although parking costs are high given its proximity to the town centre. There are disabled parking bays available, and the centre also has dedicated disabled changing, toilet and shower facilities, an access lift and hoists.

We don't have an image of Aqua Vale Pool, but here are some photos of another local pool to whet your appetite.

Above: *Wycombe Rye Lido, Buckinghamshire*

CHESHAM MOOR GYM AND SWIM

ENGLAND Buckinghamshire

Chesham Moor Gym and Swim
Moor Road, Chesham
Buckinghamshire
HP5 1SE

- ctcpool@chesham.gov.uk
- 01494 776975
- cheshammoorfitness.org.uk
- @cheshammoorgym
- @Cheshammoor
- @cheshammoorgymandswim

- 25 m x 10 m
- Council run
- Year round
- Heated
- Freshwater
- Free parking available on site
- On-site café

Chesham Moor is a fine example of a real rarity outside London – a heated outdoor pool that is open full time, year round.

It sits alongside gym facilities, so the buildings that front the pool are contemporary and purposeful. Some original charm is retained where the pool is concerned, however, by the use of baskets to store your clothes. When changing you pop your things into the basket and carry it poolside, where racks await to hold the baskets while you swim. Baskets used to be a staple of indoor and outdoor swimming pools alike, but they are now few and far between so this blast from the past feels like a treat at Chesham Moor – an unexpected treat at that, given the modern functionality of the rest of the facility.

And, really, modern functionality is what this pool is all about. It's not likely to be the sort of pool that swimmers will have on their bucket list. It doesn't really lend itself to being a day-trip destination as there isn't much space around the pool for lounging about with a book after a swim, and picnicking here would feel quite odd. But as an example of a successful, useful, workaday outdoor pool of the sort that we would all love to have within easy reach, Chesham Moor is hard to beat. It is open seven days a week with extensive hours, it is reliably warm and clean, the staff are friendly and helpful and it is well maintained. It is a faithful friend to those who live near enough to be regulars.

Don't immediately dismiss it for a lido road trip, however. It isn't grand but a visit is still very worthwhile. If you are lucky you may even see red kites wheeling overhead if you spend a little time floating on your back and drinking in the sky.

There is a short, level walk to the pool from the car park, with ramped access to reception. Once on-site access is level and spacious. There is no hoist, but there are gently sloping steps, with handrail, into the shallow end.

WYCOMBE RYE LIDO

ENGLAND Buckinghamshire

Wycombe Rye Lido
The Rye (off Bassetbury Lane),
High Wycombe
Buckinghamshire
HP11 1QX

- Wrl-sales@fusion-lifestyle.com
- 01494 769472
- fusion-lifestyle.com/centres/wycombe-rye-lido
- @WycombeRyeLido
- @WycombeRyeLido
- @wycombe_rye_lido

- 33 m x 12.5 m
- Corporately run on behalf of the council
- Year round
- Heated
- Freshwater
- Pay and display car park on site
- On-site café

This pool bears a more than passing similarity, in terms of the style of the buildings, to Brockwell, Parliament Hill and Charlton. It sits in recreation grounds with an aggressively enforced automatic-number-plate-recognition, pay-as-you-go car park. Don't risk not paying, and make sure you keep your ticket for some time after you leave; the system isn't infallible, as one of us found out to our cost.

The pool, corporately run for the local authority, is heated year round, although during the winter months you are unlikely to find the toddler pool open for business. In the summer, however, that pool is a fine addition for smaller swimmers, and the grassed areas and bleacher-style seating backing onto the buildings are well suited to lingering.

There is a gym that borders the shallow end of the pool, and

sometimes when the doors are open the music that emanates won't be to everyone's taste, so do consider packing earplugs if you prefer to swim without the pounding bass of an exercise class as a backdrop. This is only likely to be an issue when the weather is warm.

The 33-metre tank has been refurbished in recent years, and the jaunty red piping around the edge of the pool is a distinctive visual feature. Underwater lighting has been installed, and we highly recommend taking the time to visit this pool after dark. As the light hits your bubbles the tips of your fingers and feet will seem to explode in a shower of diamonds. It's a spectacular thing to watch. There are always some lanes in at Wycombe Rye, so it is a reliable choice for those of you to whom swimming lengths matters. For those who prefer a dip and a bob there's plenty of space for that too.

The changing rooms and café area lack personality, as is typical of corporate-run pools, but they are spotless. The changing areas also benefit from being warm in winter, and there is a sauna for which no extra charge is made. They are spacious, accessible by a ramp (as is the poolside) and there are solid steps, with a handrail, into the shallow end.

JESUS GREEN LIDO

ENGLAND Cambridgeshire

Jesus Green Lido
Chesterton Road, Cambridge
Cambridgeshire
CB4 3AX

- Via form on website
- 01223 302579
- better.org.uk/leisure-centre/cambridge/jesusgreenlido
- @JesusGreenLido
- @jesusgreenoutdoorpool
- @jesusgreenlido

- 90 m x 14 m
- Corporately run on behalf of the council
- Seasonal
- Unheated
- Freshwater
- On-street parking
- On-site café

This is the longest lido in the UK. Built in 1923, this historic unheated pool is over 90 metres long. As such it's a great place to lose yourself in metronomic ploughing up and down. It is truly one of the grand outdoor swimming pools of the UK, and yet because it is very unassuming it isn't usually one to feature at the top of outdoor swim lists. It has a dedicated following of local people, however, and is run by Better, which also operates a number of other open-air swimming pools in the south east of the UK.

Situated by the River Cam in the city centre, you could walk past this lido and not really know it was there; you need to cross the river by a small pedestrian bridge to reach it. Apparently built to mimic the river by being long and narrow, it is surrounded by

trees and has a pleasant area to sit around the pool on a warm day. Although you might not see it straight away, you'll hear the shrieks of people enjoying jumping into the refreshing blue water. This is a pool where people swim for fun, exercise and to cool off. It is worth emphasising that a 90-metre unheated pool can inevitably be a bit chilly – the temperature in midsummer can rise to the low twenties centigrade, but in the early days of the season it is likely to be low to mid-teens. Like the similarly lengthy pools at Tooting Bec, Newbury and Hilsea, it is a source of joy to swim this long-course pool, but entry into it can be a bit brisk even on the warmest days.

The changing rooms here are poolside cabins and there is the option of lockers or the very traditional basket room, with a rubber band for your wrist, making this feel a particularly quaint outdoor swim, redolent of the years that it has been here. There are accessible changing and toilet facilities for disabled swimmers, and a poolside hoist. Best to arrive on foot or by bike to this pool as parking locally is limited to on-street meter-controlled parking, and a public car park across Jesus Green; there is no dedicated parking for the pool itself, or any provision for disabled parking.

PETERBOROUGH LIDO

ENGLAND Cambridgeshire

Peterborough Lido
Bishop's Road, Peterborough
Cambridgeshire
PE1 1YY

- lido@vivacity-peterborough.com
- 01733 864761
- vivacity.org/vivacity-venues/peterborough-lido
- @Pboro_Lido
- @pborolido
- @peterborolidofriends

- 50 m x 18 m
- Corporately run on behalf of the council
- Seasonal
- Heated
- Freshwater
- Parking available on site
- On-site café

Peterborough Lido is little short of breathtaking. As you approach it through ornamental gardens, the exotic architecture of the place dominates the view. This is the kind of building that promises great things, experiences on a scale as grand as the setting.

There's a fear, of course, that the pools couldn't live up to the façade, that once inside, the bubble of anticipation would float skywards and out of reach. Happily, that fear is not grounded in reality, and the period mosaic tiling underfoot in the entrance is the first clue that you can expect the grandiosity of the outside to be matched inside. There are some fairly modern changing facilities that don't do justice to the rest of the facility – the garish, multicoloured locker doors jar against the muted and tasteful green of the render and the rich dark green of gloss paint built up through years of care and maintenance. But, really, that is a small blemish on an otherwise timelessly elegant surface, and at least you are guaranteed a decent shower.

The main tank is the star of the show, its size perfectly complementing the size of the buildings that encapsulate it, but the smaller pool beyond should not be overlooked; indeed, there are smaller facilities than that second pool featuring in this book as lidos in their own right. Swimming in the main tank, taking in the surrounding grandeur as you do, is a joy. This isn't a pool with an expansive vista, but the buildings are so captivating that this doesn't seem to matter. One of the greatest pleasures of these buildings is that the rooftop sun terraces remain gloriously open to the public. Take a coffee from the kiosk after your swim and climb the stairs to stroll around the terraces. Looking down over the site, hearing the splashing and sounds of happiness ring out around the rooftops is one of the many unique joys of this fine place.

The rooftop terraces are not, sadly, accessible to wheelchair users or those who find stairs challenging, but the rest of the site caters well for disabled swimmers with dedicated changing, good level access at ground level and a hoist.

MARBURY PARK OPEN AIR POOL

ENGLAND Cheshire

Marbury Park Open Air Pool
Marbury Country Park, Comberbach,
Northwich
Cheshire
CW9 6AT

marburypool@gmail.com
07599 702903
marburypool.co.uk
@marbury_pool
@marburyswimmingpool
@marburypool

25 m x 10 m
Club
Seasonal
Unheated
Freshwater
Parking available on site
Snack kiosk

Of all the pools in this guide Marbury is the closest you get to a secret (pool) garden. Set in Marbury Country Park near Northwich, this pool offers a visual feast as well as glorious and refreshing swim.

The park is on the outskirts of Northwich and is signposted from the town centre and from Junction 10 of the M56. It is close to the Anderton Boat Lift, potentially providing an enhancement to an already lovely day out at the pool, if you have time. There is car parking at the park, just a few minutes' walk from the pool, and as you approach the pool through the park the sight of part-timbered traditional gatehouse entry to the pool raises your expectations for what lies beyond; as you catch a glimpse of the pool by the entry gate the sense of anticipation heightens.

The first thing you'll notice

is the blue strip of water and its accompanying toddler pool set in lawns and surrounded by trees and bushes. You can sit on the grass, on a bench or at a picnic table either side of your swim and enjoy a drink and ice cream from the entry kiosk, or a picnic you've brought with you. The changing facilities are consistent with this historic pool – built-in wooden huts at one end of the garden, they are a little rudimentary, and don't have dedicated provision for disabled swimmers. You'll spend only a few moments of your overall visit there, but you do need to be aware that the shower is coin operated, and if you don't put money in the meter your shower will be a cold one.

It is important to check the entry details for this pool ahead of arriving – particularly if you are travelling from some distance. It is a members' pool that also sells day tickets to occasional visitors. Members have first dibs on entry to the pool up to its capacity and day visitors may have to queue on busy days; in prolonged spells of good weather the pool can be entirely closed to day visitors.

Entry to the water is via the conventional means of the ladders at the deep end, or the broad and shallow steps featuring a handrail at the shallow end. These are ideal for swimmers who are less agile, but there is no hoist available. The bold can, of course, plunge into the refreshing, unheated water of this 25-metre pool via the glorious, old-fashioned springboard and diving

platform at the deep end. On a warm and sunny day this is the kind of pool that you just don't want to get out of – there's room for swimming up and down, looking around as you do, or repeatedly jumping off the boards at the end of the pool. (Shrieking with joy is optional, but difficult to resist.)

NANTWICH OUTDOOR BRINE POOL

ENGLAND Cheshire

Nantwich Outdoor Brine Pool
Wall Lane, Nantwich
Cheshire
CW5 5LS

- nantwich.pool@everybody.org.uk
- 01270 685590
- everybody.org.uk/centres/nsp
- @EBLeisure
- @NantwichPool

- 30 m x 15 m
- Corporately run on behalf of the council
- Seasonal
- Heated
- Saltwater
- Parking available on site
- On-site café

Given that brine is more commonly associated with tinned hot dogs and preserved olives it might be that you don't find the idea of swimming in it all that appealing. If you feel like that we strongly recommend that you pack your towel, grit your teeth, and head to Nantwich to have those preconceptions shattered.

The approach to the pool is through a thoroughly modern, and therefore rather charmless leisure centre that also contains an indoor pool. It's a perfectly clean and useful facility, it just lacks character. Your prize lies beyond all that, with the outdoor brine pool having the feel of a backyard pool on a large scale. The modern changing rooms

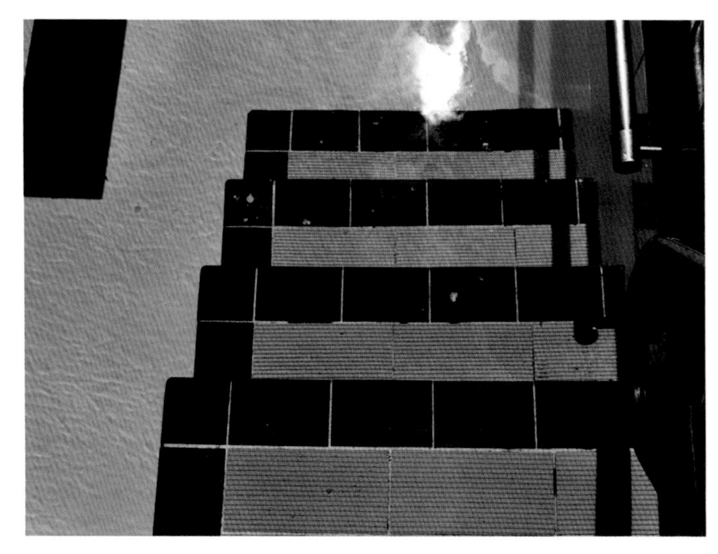

have good provision for disabled swimmers and access is level throughout the leisure centre and around the pool. Coming out of the changing rooms you'll arrive at the deep end and you'll likely notice the vintage-looking finish in the pool tank. The sunlounger, grass and kiosk area at the shallow end will beckon you to hurry along and claim your territory with scattered towels and swim bags.

If you're not keen on the idea of brine, you'll probably dither a bit, but this is the time to screw your courage to the sticking post. Wade into the shallow end down the tiled steps; dive into the deep end if you please. You will be very pleasantly surprised. The salinity of the water varies a little from session to session, so you may find that you don't notice it at all or you may find that your tongue feels a soft bite of salt. It'll never be as harshly salty as the sea. You won't come away with salt mouth or stinging eyes or crispy hair. You will come away with soft skin, and a glow that comes from having spent a few hours literally soaking up a little history. Brine pools are a rarity – there is only one other surviving in the UK at Droitwich. So savour the flavour, and embrace the brine.

It's worth timing your arrival carefully at Nantwich. This pool runs session times, and the details of these can be found on the website. The gap between the sessions can feel like a long wait if you mistime your arrival.

BUDE SEA POOL

ENGLAND Cornwall

Bude Sea Pool
Summerleaze Beach, Bude
Cornwall
EX23 8HN

- admin@budeseapool.org
- 01288 488118
- budeseapool.org
- @BudeSeaPool
- @BudeSeaPool
- @budeseapool

- Large
- Volunteer run
- Year round
- Unheated
- Saltwater
- Pay and display car parks in Bude
- In Bude

Bude Sea Pool is an ocean leviathan beached on the strand beneath the towering, layered cliffs that are a hallmark of the Culm Coast. You simply don't know it is there until you reach a point on the coast path where the stairs descend the cliff, past the terraces with pastel confectionery beach huts, to the pool. And you will walk to this pool – there is no parking immediately at hand and the walk out adds to the general sense of adventure that a visit to this pool delivers. The access, while beautiful, is not best suited to swimmers who use wheelchairs, or find a lot of stairs challenging. Once down at pool level, however, access is largely level and there is a sloping entry into the water.

Your first glimpse, as you peer over the railings at the top of the cliff, is one to be savoured. On everything other than the wildest of days the water is usually clear enough for you to see the textures and contours of the bottom of the pool through the water. This is an ocean within an ocean, a haven from the Atlantic breakers that pound this piece of coast and make it a mecca for the surfers you'll likely see beyond the sea wall of the pool when there is any swell running.

When the wind blows offshore you'll find the pool area to be delightfully sheltered; it's a proper suntrap if the sun peeps through the clouds. There is plenty of room for spreading out towels and enjoying the view of the sea beyond the pool. At high tide the sea breaches the walls, refreshing the water and making the seaward side of the pool turbulent on a rough day. If you're staying all day you'll need to make a note of high-tide times, as your picnic might well find itself claimed by the sea washing over the concrete hardstanding. Check with the lifeguards who patrol the pool in summer if you're unsure. There are some limited changing facilities and lockers in the wooden 'hub' building that sits on the terraces, but these may not be available at all times and you are most likely to be changing poolside in the open air.

The pool isn't lifeguarded in winter, but unless some sort of safety supervision is critical to you don't be put off by an out-of-season swim here. When the wind hammers onshore, battering the cliffs, it will whip across the surface off the pool and fling the spray from your arms to the sky with every stroke. The sea is particularly impressive when the winter swells roll in, and swimming in the serenity of the sea pool while listening to breakers crash beyond the walls will be a treasured experience.

HAYLE OUTDOOR SWIMMING POOL

ENGLAND Cornwall

Hayle Outdoor Swimming Pool
King George V Memorial Walk, Hayle
Cornwall
TR27 4BL

- townclerk@hayletowncouncil.net
- 01736 752568
- hayleswimmingpoolfriends.org.uk
- @HayleSwimmingPool

- 25 m x 12.5 m
- Council run in partnership with volunteers
- Seasonal
- Unheated
- Freshwater
- Free parking at the entrance at the end of King George V Memorial Walk
- On-site café

This large, freshwater, unheated pool is the sort of destination lido where you can stay all day and alternate between spending time in the spacious and grassy environment and in the pool. It is less than 10 miles from the Jubilee Pool in Penzance and, together with Bude Sea Pool, they are the only three outdoor pools in the sunny county of Cornwall. Somehow, having travelled past nineteen pools in Devon on your way to Cornwall, you'd expect there to be more. But there aren't. The ones that are here are really worth it, though.

You can see a large, hand-painted sign for Hayle Outdoor Swimming Pool shouting 'LIDO' as you travel along the B3301, a short turn-off from the A30 dual carriageway. This creates a sense of anticipation that is heightened once you catch sight of the top of the four-lane slide that deposits you

into the shallow end of the pool.

Run by Hayle Town Council, in conjunction with the Friends of Hayle Outdoor Swimming Pool, this lido is for locals and visitors alike. It is a great pool for laps and good long swims, and it's easy to keep an eye on any younger swimmers who might prefer zipping down the slides. There are steps with a handrail into the pool, but no hoist for disabled swimmers.

The individual changing rooms at the pool are big enough, while the changing block is compact. There is plenty of free parking in the nearby open car park. One of the joys of this pool is the café by the entrance; it serves both pool users and passers-by alike. Outdoor tables, plus those inside the wooden summerhouse, provide space to sit and reflect on why more people don't know about this lovely pool, which makes an ideal lido road trip in combination with any of the pools in Devon as well as the iconic Jubilee Pool in Penzance.

It's important to note that this pool runs on a cash-only basis.

JUBILEE POOL

ENGLAND Cornwall

Jubilee Pool
Battery Road, Penzance
Cornwall
TR18 4FF

- None
- 01736 369224
- jubileepool.co.uk
- @JubileePoolPZ
- @jubileepool
- @jubileepool

- 60 m x 25 m
- Volunteer run
- Seasonal
- Heated
- Saltwater
- Pay and display car park across the road
- On-site café

Pledger pic: *Sally Wood*

Humanity's resilience against the elements is hallmarked by a dogged persistence to overcome our inherent fragility. Nowhere is this more in evidence than Jubilee Pool, a gleaming white shard reclaimed from the Atlantic Ocean where it beats against the very tip of England. The engineering behind this haven for swimmers is doubly impressive for having seen a phoenix-like resurrection from the ashes of a devastating winter storm that, in 2014, overcame the staunch sea defences and caused considerable damage. For a time it seemed that the pool would be lost, and it lay battered, bruised and unusable. Significant funding grants made the restoration possible, and the engineering has been strengthened further with the tank being anchored to rock below.

The result is a crisp, pristine and architecturally magnificent triangular pool. The angles of the terraces, changing cubicles and steps into the tank converge everywhere the eye alights, and on a sunny day the shadows flung by the architecture become works of art. The steps down to the pool form an integral part of the architecture, and in the past have made disabled access challenging. However, wheelchair users can now access the site via the café entrance, and a ramp has been installed to provide access to pool level, where there is a hoist to assist with entering the water.

The seawater that fills both the small pool and the main pool is not heated, but it is filtered. There is a major project under way to separate and heat a section of the pool using geothermal energy. While the majority of the pool will remain unheated this warm pool within a pool is an exciting development.

Jubilee Pool blends the feeling of sea and pool. You'll feel flung back in time, to the heyday of the great British seaside holiday, with the gulls wheeling overhead; you'll feel somewhat cocooned inside the fortress sea defences with little sense of what beats against the outside of the walls. Remind yourself of the world beyond the walls though, by going to the top of the terraces and looking across to St Michael's Mount and the broader vista of the bay. Perhaps take a snack from the café with you. Sit awhile. Reflect on the vision and hard labour that saw this pool built at all, and marvel at the resilience that meant it was saved after the storm. Jubilee Pool is a true triumph of people against adversity, and a swim here will send you away feeling as though a little of that strength has soaked into your bones.

STANHOPE OPEN AIR POOL

ENGLAND County Durham

Stanhope Open Air Pool
Castle Park, Stanhope
County Durham
DL13 2LU

- info@stanhopepool.co.uk
- 01388 528466
- stanhopepool.co.uk
- @stanhopepool
- @stanhopepool
- @stanhopepool

- 25 m x 13 m
- Volunteer run
- Seasonal
- Heated
- Freshwater
- Parking available on site
- Snack kiosk

We're very clear that this is a book about lidos and open-air pools, and the opportunity they provide to swim outside in the UK. But it is a rare lido tourist (if we can claim that phrase?) who goes to a location purely for the swimming experience. Indeed, if it was *only* about the swim we'd all just find our most local outdoor pool, get a season ticket and swim there as often as we could (this is a great idea, by the way, and we fully support anyone who does this in between lido road trips – we certainly do!).

That's why it is worth mentioning that, like a trip to Buckfastleigh in Devon, a swim at Stanhope Pool in the beautiful North Pennines can also be a great day out on its own or together with a journey along a heritage railway. The Weardale Railway was brought back to life by tireless fundraising and volunteer hours. Likewise, Stanhope Pool is a volunteer-run community pool relying on users and fundraising to make it viable and keep the pool heating on.

Situated in the centre of Stanhope, with parking close by, this pool has the treat of both a slide and a springboard. Indoor changing rooms are found in the building you enter through, as is the snack kiosk. Outside the kiosk is café-style seating, and a small soft-play area for smaller children. There are plenty of places to sit around the pool, with an ample supply of sunloungers. On a hot day there is the shade of trees, and on cooler days there is a sauna available to enjoy. Uniquely, it is wood fired so if you want to use it mention it to the staff when you first arrive so that they can light the fire. There are disabled parking spaces at the pool, and a ramp into the building. There are dedicated disabled bathroom facilities and sloping steps, with handrails, into the water.

The drive to and from the pool across the North Pennines is spectacular and it is really worth a visit – perhaps on a lido road trip with other pools in North Yorkshire, Northumberland or Cumbria? Stanhope pool is looking a little tired at present – but please don't let that put you off. There is a great community feel, the staff are friendly and helpful, the filter coffee is excellent and pools need income in order to make improvements.

ASKHAM SWIMMING POOL

ENGLAND Cumbria

Askham Swimming Pool
Askham
Cumbria
CA10 2PN

askhampools@outlook.com
01931 712187
askhamandhelton.co.uk/swimming-pool-2
@Askhampool
@askhamswimmingpool.askham

- 20 m x 10 m
- Council run
- Seasonal
- Heated
- Freshwater
- Parking available on site
- Snack kiosk

If visiting the Lake District you are likely to have packed your walking boots, but we recommend you also pack a selection of swimming costumes. Cumbria has a nice cluster of village pools, five within a 15-mile radius of Penrith, and the open-air heated swimming pool at Askham is one of them.

This 20-metre pool is gently heated to take off the chill, with a toddler pool with stepped entry to it allowing length swimming and fun to happen alongside each other.

The pool is surrounded by places to sit on the grass and benches on which to enjoy an ice cream from the on-site kiosk,

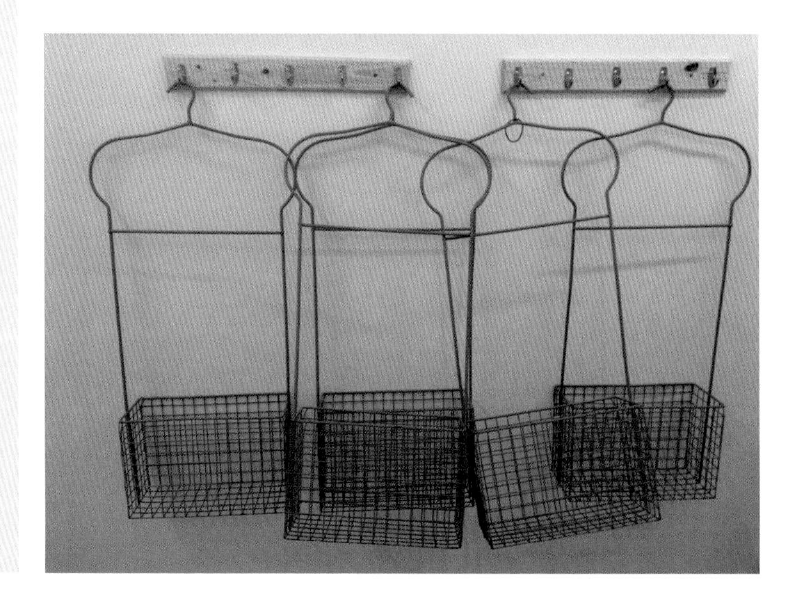

which doubles as the reception to the pool. You can bring a picnic and stay here all afternoon, as the pool is typically only open after lunch.

Changing rooms for the pool are separate male and female communal spaces with a shower in the corner of the changing room (although you have to buy a token for the shower from reception to get warm water). There is level access to the changing facilities, and a dedicated disabled toilet. Entry to the main pool is via ladders, with steps into the toddler pool.

Askham is a lovely swim in a nice setting with a warm welcome. It is also the swimming pool that we've come across with the most written instructions and A4 laminated pieces of information outside the pool and in the changing rooms – so there is always something to read!

Parking is available in an adjacent free car park. You could easily combine a swim here with a visit to other Cumbrian pools, and some time spent enjoying the many leisure attractions of the Lake District.

GREYSTOKE POOL

ENGLAND Cumbria

Greystoke Pool
Church Road, Greystoke, Penrith
Cumbria
CA11 0TW

- None
- 017684 83637
- greystokepool.org.uk
- @GreystokePool
- Greystoke & District Swimming Pool (Public Group)

- 18 m x 10 m
- Volunteer run
- Seasonal
- Heated
- Freshwater
- Parking available on site
- Snack kiosk

Each of the Cumbria pools is run as an independent community swimming pool, and though they are remarkably similar, each has a distinct personality and village setting. Greystoke Pool is right in the heart of the village. Across the road from the church and on the edge of a playground and park this community heated pool is 18 metres long, and like all the pools in this potential Cumbria lido road trip it is open in the summer months only. It is run entirely by volunteers, and sustained by entrance fees and fundraising.

This means that when visiting Greystoke Pool you definitely have to ring ahead and check that it is going to be open for you to swim in. It is a lovely pool, and a suntrap on a warm day, but you might just find it closed even on a summer bank holiday if the weather is less than perfect and there are no other swimmers.

The pool is a standard 18-metre rectangular pool with a much smaller paddling pool to one side. Changing rooms sit in the brick building that also forms the reception and kiosk space. There is limited provision for disabled swimmers, but the poolside area is level.

If you have a little time to spend in Greystoke before or after your swim you could very happily enjoy a cuppa and a slice (or two!) of a variety of cakes at the Greystoke Cycle Café, within walking distance of the pool

and signposted from the centre of the village. You can leave your car behind in the village's free car park. We mention and support the Greystoke Cycle Café for a couple of reasons – firstly, it is lovely and you'll get a warm welcome to sit in the tea garden if you come at the weekend. The second reason is that Annie, who owns and runs this café (and the accompanying 'Quirky Workshops'), is a very keen outdoor swimmer and will gladly indulge in some swimming chat with you... not least because her family used to own Kimpton Pool Club in Hertfordshire when she was young; these days she is a lake swimmer.

There's much more to Greystoke than meets the eye.

HUNSONBY SWIMMING POOL

ENGLAND Cumbria

Hunsonby Swimming Pool
Hunsonby, Penrith
Cumbria
CA10 1PN

- None
- None
- None
- Hunsonby Swimming Club

- 15 m x 6 m
- Volunteer run
- Seasonal
- Heated
- Freshwater
- Limited parking on site; parking available in the village
- Snack kiosk

The sense of anticipation of a swim at Hunsonby, north-east of Penrith, is heightened by the way in which you can see the pool as you drive towards it. Built on a corner, and surrounded by both open space and village buildings, the pool is fenced to waist height with open, traditional metal fencing. The gates are not locked, and even if they were it would be no great challenge to hop over the fence.

This means, effectively, that the pool is always available to swim in and there is an honesty box located on the wall by the small, basic changing rooms with a sign giving prices. Please make sure you use it, as income is vital to this pool's survival. There is a snack kiosk that is sometimes open when a volunteer is on duty, but this relatively small pool, with a paddling pool sited at one end, is surrounded by places to sit, picnic and enjoy the sun – so do bring a flask and some snacks.

Access to the pool from the car park is level. If the limited free parking next to the pool is taken, however, it will be necessary to park in the village and walk to the pool. There are solid steps into the shallow end, but no handrail or hoist.

This is one of those pools that really makes you wonder how a community of this size can sustain an open-air swimming pool in its centre when so very many pools in larger urban centres have just disappeared, ostensibly though lack of use. The absence of paid staff (there are no lifeguards on duty), the basic infrastructure and the volunteer-run model all, undoubtedly, help to keep costs down. If this is one stop on a Cumbria lido road trip you may be considering similar themes, and you'll have noticed how different each of these pools is. Hunsonby is, in some ways unique among landlocked pools. This open-access, relaxed, come-as-you-please model is common for sea pools where restricting access is hard or impossible. But it is unique among publicly accessible land-locked pools. And Hunsonby is all the more special for it.

SHAP SWIMMING POOL

ENGLAND Cumbria

Shap Swimming Pool
Gayle Avenue, Shap, Penrith
Cumbria
CA10 3NS

- info@shapswimmingpool.co.uk
- 07512 466172
- shapswimmingpool.co.uk
- @shappool
- @shapswimmingpool

- 16.5 m x 10 m
- Volunteer run
- Seasonal
- Heated
- Freshwater
- Small, free car park on site; additional on surrounding streets
- Snack kiosk

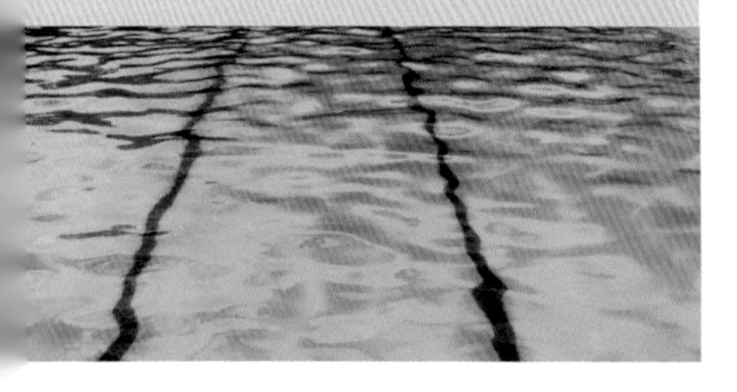

Shap Summit is the highest point on the M6, and you usually pass it at speed heading between the Lake District and Scotland. If you've got a spare hour on this journey in the summer we'd highly recommend a very small detour to Shap's lido – at an altitude of over 900 feet above sea level, it is the highest swimming pool in the UK. This guide has featured several pools directly at sea level, so it is great to be able to include one so far above!

The pool is well signposted from the main road into Shap and parking is available right outside the pool. Entry to the pool doubles as the snack kiosk and faces on to a small park of swings and slides and, rather unusually, is less than 100 metres away from the main train line between London and Glasgow, where you can intermittently see (and hear!) trains moving at speed.

There are the familiar separate male and female communal changing rooms, and thanks to a £100,000 refurbishment in the winter of 2017/2018 separate disabled changing and toilets have been created. They lead straight on to the sheltered, walled 16.5-metre swimming pool, warmed to take the chill off the water. There are semicircular steps, with a full-length handrail giving access to the shallow end, and access all around the site is level.

This is one of those pools that is run and sustained by local volunteers, members of the community and visitors; best to give them a call to make sure that they are going to be open when you plan to visit. If you get the chance to swim here, in the heart of the dramatic North Lakes scenery, it's a swim you'll remember – not least because you swam at the highest publicly accessible pool in the UK!

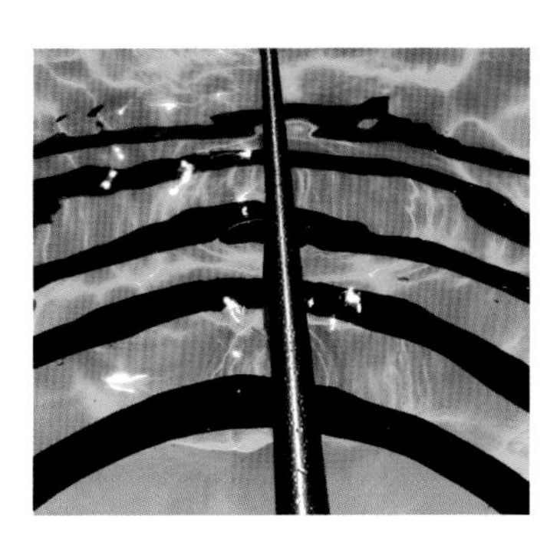

LAZONBY POOL

ENGLAND Cumbria

Lazonby Pool
Lazonby, Penrith
Cumbria
CA10 1BL

- info@lazonbypool.co.uk
- 01768 898346
- lazonbypool.co.uk
- @lazonbypool
- Lazonby Swimming Pool (Public Group)
- @lazonbyswimmingpool

- 17 m x 8 m
- Volunteer run
- Seasonal
- Heated
- Freshwater
- Parking available on site
- Snack kiosk

This is one of only a handful of open-air pools in the UK that we've found with an adjacent campsite, making it the perfect place to stay overnight and then enjoy an early-morning swim in a heated lido within yards of your bed. It also sits alongside a picturesque river. Who could ask for anything more? Greystoke Pool has a lovely B&B right next to the playing fields and pool, but camping at Lazonby is one better!

This attractive open-air pool sits in the heart of the village with ample free car parking around it – the small lane to the left of the pool is the track to the campsite and it opens out into a field where cars can be parked. The pool itself is 17 metres long with a smaller toddler pool alongside as well as a feature fountain. It is heated to a nice warm temperature, open during the summer season and is the perfect place to have a swim and enjoy conversation with locals and visitors alike. There are benches alongside the pool at which to sit pre- and post-swim, and covered seating areas too.

The changing rooms for the pool also serve the campsite, with hot showers and toilets, and they are disabled accessible. The area around the pool is level, but entry to the pool is via ladders and you need to step up over raised coping to use them. There is no hoist. The pool buildings enclose a kiosk selling drinks, sweets and hot and cold snacks to pool users and campers alike. There is also a range of local shops nearby, including Bells bakery, which supplies bread and cakes to stores throughout the north-west.

This makes a great place to start or end a Cumbrian lido road trip, and four out of the five Cumbrian pools have worked together with Eden District Council to publish details about all of the pools for visitors in the Eden's Rural Outdoor Swimming Pools leaflet. It is great to see these local initiatives encouraging swimmers to take a tour around all of the pools – after all their hard work, it would be rude not to, really.

So, can you swim all of the Cumbrian pools in a day? You'd have to plan that lido road trip quite carefully, and ring in advance to make sure that they were all open at the times you planned to swim. It is probably more doable in two days – particularly if you can grab an early-morning swim at Lazonby after spending the night before in their campsite.

HATHERSAGE SWIMMING POOL

ENGLAND Derbyshire

Hathersage Swimming Pool
Oddfellows Road, Hathersage
Derbyshire
S32 1DU

- info@hathersageswimmingpool.co.uk
- 01433 650843
- hathersageswimmingpool.co.uk
- @HathersageSwimmingPool

- 33 m x 10 m
- Volunteer run
- Year round
- Heated
- Freshwater
- Limited parking on site; pay and display car park across the road
- On-site café

There can be few experiences in life that offer quite as much visceral pleasure as a piping-hot shower after a glorious swim taken under the sky with one's gaze held robustly by the hills beyond. Throw into that view a Victorian bandstand sitting poolside and you've got a very heady mix that makes Hathersage hard to beat in terms of lido experiences, even before you consider the modern indoor changing rooms that are a nice counterpoint to the period shelter on the opposite side of the pool.

This pool has gone from strength to strength since being taken into community stewardship relatively recently in its lengthy history, and now offers one of the longest heated seasons in the country. They've achieved this despite being situated in a small town in the Peak District

with a correspondingly small local population. That always represents a challenge for pools, as they rely on locals to keep the pool afloat on those run-of-the-mill weather days that don't produce long queues and their associated income. It's also fair to say that the Peak District climate doesn't lend itself to delivering many of those hot days that have people queuing around the block. However, spectacular weather doesn't always have to mean brilliant sunshine. The delightful photographs of the pool surrounded by snow, or the dragon's breath gently rising from the warm water that feature on the pool's social media channels in the winter months, testify to that!

The secret, if we can call it that, to Hathersage's success is imagination and passion on the part of the largely volunteer body of people involved with running it. They offer an impressive range of events and special swims, with perhaps the cream of the crop being the night-time swims with live music playing from the bandstand. These sell out quickly, so pre-booking is essential. Events like this draw people from far and wide, bringing the much-needed income that is vital to any pool's sustainability. And Hathersage has a keen eye on sustainability, recognising the value of solar power to both reduce their costs and make an environmental difference.

Even without a special event to attend this is a pool that will richly reward the lido road tripper, and not just with the swimming and the views. The café underneath the pool is a treat, so do build in time for a visit. It's very popular with cyclists on a weekend morning through the year, so be prepared for a crowd on busy mornings, but the breakfast will be worth the wait.

There is a short flight of steps up to the pool entrance, but the poolside area itself offers level access to the pool and changing rooms. Access to the tank is via ladders.

ASHBURTON SWIMMING POOL

ENGLAND Devon

Ashburton Swimming Pool
Whistley Hill, Love Lane, Ashburton
Devon
TQ13 7DW

- info@ashburtonpool.com
- 01364 652828
- ashburtonpool.com
- @ASHBURTON_POOL
- @ashburtonswimmingpool

- 21 m x 9 m
- Volunteer run
- Seasonal
- Heated
- Freshwater
- Town car park five minutes' walk away
- Snack kiosk

The ancient stannary town of Ashburton feels like an unlikely home for an outdoor pool. Its higgledy-piggledy array of period buildings lends it an air of genteel quaintness, and the urge to wander a while and explore it will be strong. Which is just as well, as you'll need to do a little exploring to find this pool, tucked away off the high street around five minutes' walk from the car park in the centre of town. On a busy day you'll be able to follow the sound of excited shrieking and whooping that is very often the first sign that you are nearing a lido. If in doubt, stop a passer-by and ask for directions.

Once you have tracked your quarry, however, you can't help but be charmed by the heated Ashburton Swimming Pool. It sits on a pretty suntrap of a site, with plenty of grassy space for picnics. The changing rooms and bathrooms are charmingly rustic; none of your bland corporate veneer here. Recently taken under community control, there is a kiosk where you can fill your tummies, and if you're lucky there will be home-made cakes from a volunteer.

The pool doesn't lend itself readily to length swimming, with a scalloped cut-out in the shallow end providing stepped access that, even without a handrail, is very helpful for children and those with reduced mobility (who will also benefit from level access all around the pool area). But if you're adaptable, and can live without a tumble turn at times, then the pool is plenty long enough for a decent swim.

In our view, though, it is best suited for a family day out and it lies so close to a number of other Devon pools that you can readily have a double-dip lido road trip. Maybe even a treble dip, if you time it right...

BOVEY TRACEY SWIMMING POOL

ENGLAND Devon

Bovey Tracey Swimming Pool
Newton Road, Bovey Tracey, Newton Abbot
Devon
TQ13 9BD

- boveypool@gmail.com
- 01626 832828
- boveyswimmingpool.org.uk
- @boveypool
- @BoveyPool

- 25 m x 9 m
- Volunteer run
- Seasonal
- Heated
- Freshwater
- Satnav users should follow TQ13 9FF; Off-road parking within recreation ground off Newton Road, or on surrounding roads
- Snack kiosk

Bovey is a surprise and a delight. It is easy to miss it altogether, as although your satnav will take you to a road that runs alongside it the sign itself is hard to spot. Your landmark is the recreation ground – if you have found that, you have found the pool. Walk along the boundary wall towards what will look like fairly uninspiring pavilion buildings and look out for the path that leads to them.

If the exterior of Bovey Tracey looks uninspiring from the road, we can promise you that the interior is anything but.

You'll enter, having paid your admission to a volunteer, and be directed past a basket store, also manned by volunteers. The changing rooms are functional and clean, but the best is very much yet to come.

When you step through the door to poolside, you'll be greeted by a pool that is bigger than you're expecting it to be, given the understated nature of the entrance, flanked by trees and terraced seating. You'll look around and notice a raised toddler pool, helpfully situated at the end of that seating. What is most likely to strike you next are the wonderful wall mosaic artworks that are such a striking feature of this pool. They stand as evidence of the community love that goes into this place. The people here are unfailingly friendly, and lido chat seems to come easily to them whatever their ages. It's a pool well used by locals, but it never feels exclusive or unwelcoming.

This isn't a huge site, but on those busy hot days the numbers are well managed and you don't feel overwhelmed. People rub along nicely, good manners are much in evidence and the staff and volunteers are tolerant, warm and helpful. On more lacklustre days this pool is a heated pleasure, and the water is just a couple of steps from the changing-room door, so don't be put off by a bit of cloud or rain.

The poolside area is mainly level, and access into the pool itself is by way of ladders only. There is no hoist, and that may make it less than ideal for wheelchair users.

BUCKFASTLEIGH OPEN AIR POOL

ENGLAND Devon

Buckfastleigh Open Air Pool
Victoria Park, Buckfastleigh
Devon
TQ11 0DB

- bfl.pool@yahoo.co.uk
- 01364 642222
- buckfastleighpool.co.uk
- @bflpool
- @victoriaparkbuckfastleigh

- 21 m x 10 m
- Volunteer run
- Seasonal
- Heated
- Freshwater
- Pay and display car park and on-street parking
- Snack kiosk

Buckfastleigh is one of the oldest pools featured in this book, and its survival in a town that does not entirely match the affluent economic profile of much of the surrounding area is nothing short of remarkable. Underinvested in, crumbling and destined for permanent closure by the local authority, the pool was saved when the community rallied round, as have so many communities across the country.

They were successful in taking the pool into community stewardship in 2015, and the story of how they got there brings a tear to the eye over the sheer grit and dogged persistence of the campaign. The result is a sweet pool. It's not quite the full 25 metres, but it still lends itself to a good solid distance swim during lane sessions. It is unsurprisingly popular with families during general swimming sessions, not least as it sits in a newly refurbished park featuring a new skate park and obstacle

equipment. The saving of this pool has led to a wholesale regeneration of the entire park, which is a much-needed facility for the youth of the town.

Lido road trippers will love it too, however. The pool itself sits in a tiny footprint, which limits its site capacity and therefore its income. There is some elevated terracing on the roof of the building, which offers a nice spot to spread out a towel and watch the action in the pool, as well as giving a view of the park. Lido road trippers are vital to the sustainability of this pool. If you are heading south for a holiday this pool is an ideal stop-off point en route to Cornwall,

being just a couple of minutes off the A38, with parking right outside. There are drinks and snacks available, with reception doubling as a snack kiosk, and the indoor changing rooms retain some original charm while also boasting newly refurbished shower and toilet facilities, so you can get on your way feeling refreshed in many ways. It's worth pressing on from Exeter services for, without a doubt, and while predominantly seasonal, it also offers unheated swimming on winter weekend mornings, and for the last couple of years has offered heated swimming around the festive period. If you're planning a winter visit, do check the opening arrangements before setting out.

Access to the pool building is level from the car park. The corridor around the changing rooms is quite tight for wheelchair manoeuvrability, but not impossible. There are, however, three or four steps up to the poolside area and access to the pool is via ladders only. Without a hoist these things may combine to make this pool less than ideally accessible for swimmers with significantly reduced mobility.

CHAGFORD SWIMMING POOL

ENGLAND Devon

Chagford Swimming Pool
Rushford, Chagford, Newton Abbot
Devon
TQ13 8DA

- info@chagfordpool.co.uk
- 01647 432929
- chagfordpool.co.uk
- @chagfordpool
- @ChagfordSwimmingPool
- @chagfordpool

- 33 m x 17 m
- Volunteer run
- Seasonal
- Heated
- Freshwater
- Limited parking on site; public car park in the village
- Snack kiosk

This volunteer-run pool is a gem. Heated by solar panels, it is river fed and is plenty big enough for a really decent swim and a cuppa from the kiosk afterwards. Although not in the centre of the village of Chagford, it is a relatively easy pool to find even if the approach roads are a little on the narrow side.

There is a free car park next to the river to access the pool, with overflow parking available in a field to add to the rustic charm. If that fills up park in the village and walk down. There is no dedicated disabled parking, but passengers can be dropped off right outside. There is an accessible bathroom for disabled swimmers, and the site is level throughout, with sloping access to the water.

Chagford has what may well qualify as one of prettiest settings for an outdoor pool there is. It is completely rural,

surrounded by trees and birds, and the gentle burble of the river can be heard when it is not drowned out by the noise of happy swimmers.

In addition to the glorious swim at this pool there are several other things about a visit here that will bring a smile to your face. Two particular favourites are the

rack of assorted wetsuits that sit alongside the changing rooms, which you can hire/borrow for a small donation, and the bookcase of novels that you can borrow or buy to read while at the pool or to take away with you. These may seem like small things, but they show that the volunteers running the pool think hard about what would enhance a visit here; it's evidence of the kind of caring, nurturing approach that is needed to sustain volunteer-run pools.

The volunteers have worked hard to raise money to improve the facilities over the years; the pool wasn't always heated, but now it reaches the giddy heights of 24°C! Yet while introducing a touch of modernity they have retained a sense of tradition in keeping with a pool that has been here for decades. It was dug by hand in 1933, and you get a strong sense that this is a pool that has been passed through generations of volunteers and swimmers – just like the wetsuits handed on by those who have swum here.

CHUDLEIGH COMMUNITY POOL

ENGLAND Devon

Chudleigh Community Pool
Lawn Drive, Chudleigh, Newton Abbot
Devon
TQ13 0LS

- ccp@chudleighpool.org.uk, admin@chudleighpool.org.uk
- 01626 852147
- chudleighpool.org.uk
- @ccpChudleighPool

- 25 m x 10 m
- Volunteer run
- Seasonal
- Heated
- Freshwater
- Car park and on-street parking
- Snack kiosk

This is a community pool situated next to a school, and you need to pass through the school car park to find it. As you approach the school building look to the left and you will see the fencing that surrounds the pool. Follow your nose around the side of the building and you'll reach the entrance. It is run by volunteers and is a decent width 25-metre pool where you can enjoy a good swim – particularly during the adult-only sessions held in the early morning. It is great for families as well at other times of day, and there is a very useful covered area where you can leave your things, or eat your picnic, if rain threatens.

The changing rooms and showers are in the entrance block and there are paved areas around the pool for drying off or sitting in the sun on warm days. The changing facilities, which include disabled-accessible changing, can be accessed by a ramp. At the time of writing Chudleigh's hoist was no longer fit for service, and funding had been applied for to replace it. You should therefore telephone ahead to find out the current situation.

There is a kiosk within the entrance/changing block where you can buy drinks and sweets, and there is free car parking on site for a small number of cars and additional on-street parking around the pool.

CLYST HYDON SWIMMING POOL

ENGLAND Devon

Clyst Hydon Swimming Pool
Clyst Hydon, Cullompton
Devon
EX15 2NT

- None
- None
- sites.google.com/site/clysthydonswimmingclub
- @ClystHydonSwim

- 20 m x 10 m
- Volunteer run
- Seasonal
- Unheated
- Freshwater
- At the village hall in the centre of the village
- None available

This unheated 20-metre pool in a small village in Devon is truly a hidden gem. In this guide we've referred to other pools where your sense of anticipation is heightened by what you can, or can't, see on your approach. This pool reveals itself only at the very last minute, after a short walk up a wooded track that opens out into a hollow in the hills containing your prize.

This feels apt, as Clyst Hydon itself is a village off the beaten track. It takes a little bit of finding. When you get there, however, there is ample free parking at the village hall, around 150 metres from the clearly signposted gate to the swimming pool in the centre of the village. The changing rooms are rudimentary. There is no getting away from that. The pool is unheated and is definitely brisk on entry. There is no getting away from that either. But neither of these things really feel like they matter once you've taken your first plunge (or arrived in the pool via the slide) and there is space for a decent swim and lots of fun to happen alongside each other.

The community spirit is clearly strong in Clyst Hydon and the pool is part of that.

The welcome is as warm as the water is brisk. If you are in lido tourist mode, it is worth looking out on Facebook for the two or three Sundays a year that the volunteers who run this pool organise a 'pool breakfast', where they barbecue a cooked post-swim breakfast as a fundraising activity. People come from far and wide to enjoy this treat.

The pool isn't very accessible for people with limited mobility, but this is something the volunteers would like to change if funding can be secured. As things may have changed since publication of this book this is definitely a pool it will be worth calling in advance to confirm current access provision.

CORNWALL HOUSE OUTDOOR POOL

ENGLAND Devon

Cornwall House Outdoor Pool
St German's Road, Exeter
Devon
EX4 6TG

- exetersport@exeter.ac.uk
- 01392 722515
- sport.exeter.ac.uk/facilities/swimming
- @UniversityofExeterSport
- @UniversityofExeterSport

- 25 m x 10 m
- University run
- Seasonal
- Heated
- Freshwater
- Limited visitor parking on campus
- None available

There are a good number of Exeter residents who are unaware of the existence of this fine pool. It is snuggled into the heart of the university campus, and opens seasonally for heated swimming. It has the look and feel of being a members and/or students-only pool, but it is gloriously open to the public.

If you are not local to Exeter it will feel like a chore to get to. There is almost no parking nearby, but the campus is well served by public transport. Once on campus you'll need to follow signs to the pool, but even then it will be easy to go astray. Being terribly un-British and stopping a stranger to ask for directions if needed is highly recommended.

Your efforts will be worthwhile, however. The heated pool sits in a pretty grassed garden area, with spankingly modern (if few) poolside changing cubicles. There is usually a lane in, so the exerciser and dipper alike will be happy, and stretching out on a towel after a swim you'll feel as though you've found your oasis. And there are advantages to this pool being comparatively little known and difficult to find. We have yet to experience heavy queues on a hot day, although we must caveat that by saying this may be complete fluke.

There is no catering on site, but there is a small campus grocery store very close to the pool and when we have been the lifeguards have been very relaxed about letting you out to buy snacks and then readmitting you.

Swimmers with reduced mobility will need to be aware of the distance from this pool to any vehicle drop-off point, as well as the ladder-only access to the tank itself.

Cornwall House Pool
• Heated Pool
• Non-members welcome

0.9 m

DARTMOUTH OUTDOOR POOL

ENGLAND Devon

Dartmouth Outdoor Pool
Milton Lane, Dartmouth
Devon
TQ6 9HW

- dartmouthswimmingpool@gmail.com
- 0777 993 5970
- None
- facebook.com/groups/688958724647818

- 25 m x 8.5 m
- Community run
- Seasonal
- Heated
- Freshwater
- Car park and on-street parking available
- Snack kiosk

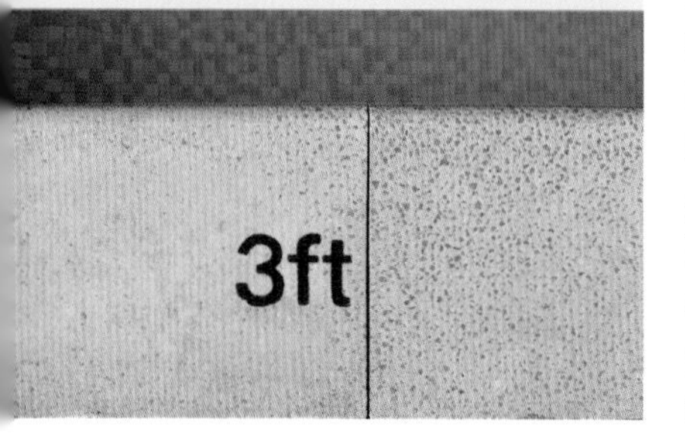

This is a glorious, heated community pool you might miss for a couple of reasons. It is has a very low profile, undeservedly so, and even some locals and long-time regular visitors to Dartmouth don't know it is there. It was faced with the threat of closure when the indoor pool up the road was opened in 2017, and the outdoor pool's location at the top of the town, next to Dartmouth Academy school, is a little out of the way. The growth of the school buildings has squeezed the pool into the corner of the campus in recent years, but outside school hours that does bring the advantage of plentiful parking as the handful of spaces belonging to the pool are reserved for staff.

Should you get the opportunity to swim here, it'll be one of those swims that sticks in your mind. The staff and volunteers who run this community pool offer a welcome as warm as the nicely heated water. The 25-metre pool is good for lengths and family fun alike, and there are grassy areas and seats for lounging and picnicking. The kiosk runs from the reception area, and has a good range of snacks.

There are separate male and female communal changing

rooms and showers, with a very effective (and novel) use of wire shopping baskets for your belongings. There are no dedicated disabled facilities, but once inside the changing areas there is plenty of space. Access into and around the site is level, and access to the tank is via ladders.

Dartmouth offers a simply lovely swim that punches well above the weight suggested by its low profile. There's the opportunity of a lido road trip with a host of other Devon pools; Salcombe, Meadowbrook, Buckfastleigh and Plymouth's Tinside and Mountwise swims would all complement a swim at Dartmouth. And if you double up with a swim at Teignmouth Lido you'll get to take the higher ferry across the River Dart if travelling by car. And who doesn't like a lido ferry trip?

KINGSTEIGNTON SWIMMING POOL

ENGLAND Devon

Kingsteignton Swimming Pool
Meadowcroft Drive, Kingsteignton,
Newton Abbot
Devon
TQ12 3PB

- kingsteigntonpool@gmail.com
- 01626 366480
- kingsteigntonswimmingpool.org.uk
- @kingsteigntonsw
- Kingsteignton Swimming Pool
- @kingsteigntonswimmingpool

- 25 m x 10 m
- Volunteer run
- Seasonal
- Heated
- Freshwater
- Free parking available on site
- Snack kiosk

A relatively modern open-air swimming pool (meaning, built in the authors' lifetime!), this lido is situated in the middle of the village with car parking available on site and a heated 25-metre strip of blue within enclosed walls.

This pool has longer opening dates than some seasonal pools, usually opening in mid- to late April; it would be great for an early season lido road trip. It is one which gets a lot of use from the local community, who also run the pool. It is typical of the rural open-air pools featured in this guide in that it serves a community of 11,000 residents (although some rural pools serve much smaller communities), yet is also available to a much wider visiting population from both near and far. By now you will have noticed how much we've mentioned the post-swim snacks and drinks, so we particularly like that the first money raised, in 1973, to build this pool was the proceeds of a coffee morning.

For a community-run pool, Kingsteignton is quite well equipped for disabled swimmers, with facilities including a hoist and accessible changing. At the time of writing, the volunteers were also working with a local organisation to provide dedicated sessions for disabled swimmers who may not have the confidence to attend regular sessions.

DEPTH

DEPTH
Fast Lane
Swim Clockwise

MEADOWBROOK POOL

ENGLAND Devon

Meadowbrook Pool
Dartington, Totnes
Devon
TQ9 6JU

- None
- None
- None
- @meadowbrookpool
- Meadowbrook Pool, Dartington Swimming Club

- 25 m x 10 m
- Volunteer run
- Seasonal
- Unheated
- Freshwater
- Pay and display car park five minutes' walk away
- Snack kiosk

Meadowbrook has fewer opening hours than many of the pools featured in this book, and in many ways, this makes swimming in it feel like a significant achievement as well as a lovely way to spend a couple of hours. It is another of those community pools that relies heavily on volunteers to operate it, and is open after school during the summer term months and a little longer on school holiday afternoons. There can, however, be short-notice changes to the timetable in poor weather, or if there are insufficient volunteers, so calling ahead is essential.

Surrounded by a high open-lattice fence, the pool is visible from the road (which is how we first discovered it when cycling from Totnes to Buckfastleigh). As it is opposite the Dartington village centre, there are several places to grab a coffee or something to eat if

you are waiting for it to open. Pay and display parking is also available here.

This wide unheated pool is 25 metres long and gives the opportunity of some good lap swimming on days when it isn't too busy. The term time/school holiday hours reflect that this pool is aimed at local children, who make good use of it and queue to get in each day in a way that warms your heart for the future of the pool.

The changing rooms are in a newly constructed wooden block across the grass from the pool and there is a snack kiosk on site to buy sweets and drinks from post-swim. The same building also houses the toilets and looks like it has seen good times as a club house in the past. There is a disabled-access toilet, but swimmers with reduced mobility would find getting in and out of the pool challenging as there are no steps or hoist.

If you get your timings right, Meadowbrook would make a good addition to a lido road trip taking in the pools at Buckfastleigh and Ashburton.

MORETONHAMPSTEAD POOL

ENGLAND Devon

Moretonhampstead Pool
Court Street, Moretonhampstead,
Newton Abbot
Devon
TQ13 8LG

- moretonpool@hotmail.co.uk
- 01647 440276
- moretonpool.co.uk
- @moretonpool
- @MoretonhampsteadSwimmingPool
- @moreton_pool

- 25 m x 10 m
- Volunteer run
- Seasonal
- Heated
- Freshwater
- In Court Street car park
- Snack kiosk

An increasing number of pools are turning to renewable energy, and nothing says 'heated water' better than a bank of solar panels at an outdoor pool. It's enough to put a spring in your step as you pick up the pace in a rush to dive in. Moretonhampstead is one such pool.

The reception desk (which doubles as the snack kiosk), changing rooms (which include disabled-accessible changing areas), and toilets are all housed in one block running alongside the length of this 25-metre pool, where the water is heated to a comfortable temperature for those who like their lidos warmed and yet still refreshing enough for the cold-water enthusiast.

The team of volunteers who run Moretonhampstead pool offer a wide variety of different sessions for different swimmer preferences, and there are opportunities for you to swim in lanes here as well as to have a cooling dip on a hot day, plus enjoying a picnic or snack in the green environs of the pool. On rainy days, however, the policy is to close the pool so if the weather looks in doubt please phone ahead to check.

With a pay and display car park adjacent to the pool and close to the centre of the village, you'll have easy access to this pool. Once in the car park, you need to look down toward the back corner to see the entrance, as the pool is obscured from view behind a hedge. Sometimes there are flags flying, which are a helpful pointer.

Access into the pool from the car park is mainly level, with a slight incline, and the changing areas and poolside are level and accessible. There is no hoist to assist with access to the water.

MOUNTWISE SWIMMING POOL

ENGLAND Devon

Mountwise Swimming Pool
James Street, Plymouth
Devon
PL1 4HG

- mountwiseinfo@everyoneactive.com
- 01752 306265
- everyoneactive.com/centre-finder/mount-wise-swimming-pools
- @eaMountWise
- @eaMountWise
- @eamountwise

- 25 m x 10 m
- Corporately run on behalf of the council
- Seasonal
- Unheated
- Saltwater
- Free on-street parking close by
- Snack kiosk

Swimming at the Mountwise open-air swimming pools complex is free. No charge. Nada. Nothing. Yes, you read that correctly. It is the stuff the authors of this book dream about – a publicly accessible open-air swimming pool, overlooking the sea, where you can park easily and swim for free. Run by leisure company Everyone Active, like the nearby iconic and historic Tinside Lido, this pool is run in conjunction with the very supportive Plymouth City Council, the aim is to get as many people locally using it as possible. As a result, the pools tend to be very busy, particularly when the sun is out and the sunloungers and deckchairs come into their own.

There are three pools at this promenade complex – a 25-metre one for swimming, a fun pool for general enjoyment and cooling off (which benefits from sloping, beach-style entry) and a paddling pool for little ones. There are disabled-accessible toilet facilities, and access in and around the pools is level although there is no hoist for the main pool.

As you sit with an ice cream or a cuppa at Mountwise, you might take a moment to reflect that Plymouth is a city of two quite different lidos. Although they are both on the coast and both unheated lovelies, one is front and centre of the city and (almost!) always features in newspaper articles on lidos. The other one – this one – is the kind of lesser-known locals' pool that you might wish you had access to on a regular basis.

0.75M

SALCOMBE SWIMMING POOL

ENGLAND Devon

Salcombe Swimming Pool
Onslow Road, Salcombe
Devon
TQ8 8AG

- None
- 07746 248187
- None
- @Salcombe.Swimming.Pool

- 25 m x 10 m
- Volunteer run
- Seasonal
- Heated
- Freshwater
- Parking available on site
- Snack kiosk

This pool feels like one you'll only know about if you are local to Salcombe, or know someone who is. Like several other open-air pools in Devon it is a local pool run by local people primarily for those who live in their community. Separate from, but situated next to, the Church of England primary school on the northern outskirts of Salcombe, it has only a handful of parking spaces outside the front door, and although there is street parking in the area, the pool is a good twenty-minute walk uphill from the centre of Salcombe.

This is a straightforward 25-metre pool heated to a very comfortable temperature and run by volunteers a few hours per day in the summer, with lots of pool inflatables and floats to borrow. The swim is good as an adult, and lengths are easily doable, although the pool is aimed mainly at a younger audience having fun in the general sessions. It has limited space around it to sit and relax in the sun and the changing rooms are pretty small, although there are showers – but, as always, this doesn't really matter if what you've come for is a swim.

There are grab handles to assist less mobile swimmers, but wheelchair access to the site is not easy. The need to improve access is very firmly on the pool's radar, however, so do call ahead before visiting if access might be an issue and they can advise you of the current situation.

The welcome here was as warm as the pool temperature, and there was plenty of choice of sweets and drinks at the kiosk run at reception for post-swim refuelling; there is also no shortage of places to eat in downtown Salcombe.

SHOALSTONE POOL

ENGLAND Devon

Shoalstone Pool
Berry Head Road, Brixham
Devon
TQ5 9FT

- info@shoalstonepool.com
- None
- shoalstonepool.com
- @shoalstonepool
- @shoalstone
- @shoalstonepool

- 53 m x 17 m
- Charitable trust run
- Seasonal
- Unheated
- Saltwater
- Parking available on site
- On-site café and snack kiosk

Any swimmer who has spent any time at all looking at swimming-related social media feeds will be familiar with the Bondi Icebergs sea pool, even if they have never set foot in Australia. We're not usually in the business of comparisons; all the pools in this book are delightfully individual. But in the case of Shoalstone the comparison is so powerful that it would be remiss not to mention it.

The pool is sunk into a concrete slab perched atop a rocky promontory at what feels like the very end of Brixham itself. You can't see the pool from the car park, or from the road as you approach. You will begin to doubt whether you are going in the right direction. But there comes a point, as you walk towards the pool, where the land falls away beneath you and you look down on a turquoise oasis. The clear seawater filters and

reflects the light off the crisp, white, painted tank. On the dullest of days this pool glows like something almost other-worldly. Your pace will quicken, and if you have ever seen a picture of Bondi Icebergs it will leap readily to mind.

Down at pool level there are some solid white period buildings standing sentinel with serried ranks of blue-doored changing cubicles spreading out like tentacles. That blue is picked up on in the pool surrounds, and the colour scheme of this pool is one of its most charming features. It perfectly

complements the ocean beauty beyond, and if you enter the pool through the gentle slope at the shallow end you'll have plenty of opportunity to savour that view.

The shallow end is so shallow that swimming a full length is a challenge; we recommend turning a little early as you approach it – particularly if you are a long-limbed front crawler. But the upside is that you can sit in the water and while away some time people watching. It also makes it perfect for small children, who can splash and play feeling very safe and well within their depth, and the sloped entry to the pool will be helpful for swimmers with reduced mobility – although the steps that pepper the rest of the site will be less smooth to navigate.

During the summer the pool is lifeguarded, and the tank cleaned out regularly. In winter the water is left to nature and swimming is not encouraged, apart from on specially advertised occasions, when any storm-tossed debris will have been removed from the tank. If you choose to swim here in winter, you do so very much at your own risk.

This pool survives on fresh air and seawater primarily, given that it remains free to use. Shoalstone does not have the advantage of a corporate operator, like Mountwise, being volunteer run. It therefore has no financial buffer, and storm damage in 2018 showed its vulnerability. Had that been any worse than it was the pool may have found it almost impossible to recover from. There is a donation box on the wall of the building, and if you enjoy your swim there – as we are confident you will – please leave a donation in the box and do your bit to help preserve this gem for the generations to come.

The upper floor of the building houses a café that has among the best views available in a lido café. This also helps to support the pool by way of rent from the tenant. Supporting the café is no chore, given that the food is as marvellous as the view. So do consider stopping for a bite to eat. You'll be doing your bit for a very worthwhile cause and your stomach will thank you for it.

TEIGNMOUTH LIDO

ENGLAND Devon

Teignmouth Lido
Eastcliff Walk, Teignmouth
Devon
TQ14 8TA

- leisure@teignbridge.gov.uk
- 01626 779063
- teignbridgeleisure.co.uk/swim
- @Teignbridge
- @teignbridgeleisure

- 25 m x 12.5 m
- Council run
- Seasonal
- Heated
- Freshwater
- Eastcliffe car park within walking distance, pay and display on-street parking nearby
- Snack kiosk

If you are working your way through this book reading about or visiting different open-air pools you might be mentally pigeonholing them into different categories. Teignmouth is one you might put into the category of 'pools with a sea view', and is as picturesque to swim in as it is to stand outside of looking out over the sea. It is a shame that the view can only be glimpsed from inside the pool by peering out through the porthole-style openings in the gates.

It is a lovely 25-metre pool surrounded by a variety of buildings and wide poolside spaces, that offer opportunities to relax afterwards with a drink or a picnic. Behind the main building, tucked out of sight, is a small play area for children. There are some vending machines and a snack kiosk on site, but the latter looks like it is not always in use and you would be well advised to bring a picnic. There is, however, a café with excellent sea views and outside seating directly opposite the pool entrance on the esplanade, should a hankering for chips and ice cream overtake you.

There are steps with a handrail accessing the pool and disabled-accessible toilets, but no hoist. The changing facilities are indoor, reasonably modern, and accessible. As it's a short walk uphill from the centre of Teignmouth and within walking distance of the train station, this is an ideal stop on a lido rail trip taking in Topsham and Cornwall House pools, both also accessible by rail. The profusion, if we can call it that, of open-air pools in Devon means that it would also make a great lido road trip with a number of nearby pools.

TINSIDE LIDO

ENGLAND Devon

Tinside Lido
Hoe Road, Plymouth
Devon
PL1 3DE

- tinsidelido@everyoneactive.com
- 01752 261915
- everyoneactive.com/centre/tinside-lido
- @eaTinside
- @eaTinsideLido

- 50 m x 25 m
- Corporately run on behalf of the council
- Seasonal
- Unheated
- Saltwater
- Parking available
- Snack kiosk

Tinside can, with some ease, stake a claim to being one of the grandest lidos in this guide. It is a jewel in Plymouth's crown, and looking at it today it is hard to imagine that it lay unused and near derelict for years before being restored and returned to public use.

It lies in the shadow of Plymouth Hoe, and the iconic red-and-white Smeaton's Tower can be seen from poolside. You enter at Hoe level, having already had your heart quicken at the massive, semicircular azure jewel laid out below you. It juts, proud and elegant, into Plymouth Sound, like the after deck of a five-star cruise liner. The tank is clean and bright, with jaunty deckchair stripes painted on the bottom and the classic fountain at its heart. As you drop down to the pool you feel as though you are descending into the belly of an Art Deco beast. There is a lift for those with limited ability to manage stairs – a very welcome modern addition – but much else remains as it was in its 1930s heyday. The vintage tiling in the stairwell is serene and graceful.

At pool level the terracing is enormous. This is a large site that can hold a lot of swimmers and sunbathers in comfort. From the seaward side of the crescent you can look back and truly appreciate the scale, and stark simplicity, of the Art Deco pavilion that houses the changing rooms. The upper floor of the pavilion remains unused at the time of writing, which is a great shame. We have heard from Plymothians that it used to be quite the place to see and be seen, and the rooftop sun terraces above it, also now dormant, were a sought-after spot on a fine day. We hope these spaces will be brought back into use at some stage, as they represent untapped income-generation potential.

It used to be possible to swim in the Sound via some steps at the seaward side of the pool, to enjoy the tamed and untamed ocean in one outing. That pleasure has long since been denied to swimmers, which is a shame, but in terms of income protection and defining liability for a lifeguarded facility one can understand why it is so.

The water is filtered and treated but unheated saltwater. This can be something of a shock to the system if you're not expecting it. The pool looks for all the world like it is filled with chlorinated freshwater, and if you hurl yourself in and get a salty mouthful when you're expecting fresh, it can make for some amusing spluttering. Amusing to your companions, at least. And this is a pool that is ideally suited to enjoying in company – its scale lends itself to big gatherings of swimmers creating a territory of towels.

TOPSHAM POOL

ENGLAND Devon

Topsham Pool
Fore Street, Topsham, Exeter
Devon
EX3 0HF

- topshampool@gmail.com
- 01392 874477
- topshampool.com
- @TopshamPool
- @TopshamOutdoorSwimmingPool

- 25 m x 10 m
- Volunteer run
- Seasonal
- Heated
- Freshwater
- Pay and display car parks next to the pool and at Topsham Quay and Holman Way
- Vending machines

If you were to make a new year's resolution to swim in more outdoor pools this year you couldn't make a better start than heading to Topsham for their New Year's Day opening. Before you cry, 'I'm not swimming in cold water on 1 January in the UK!' let us assure you that this is one of the toastiest outdoor swims in the book *even* on New Year's Day. The first session of the year is reserved for the local and appropriately named 'Nutters' group, but there are generally two other well-attended general swimming sessions on the day and they can get your lido year off to a good and refreshing start.

Situated in the centre of Topsham, the pool is a short

walk from the station and adjacent to a small pay and display car park. If that is full there is some time-limited on-street parking nearby and larger pay and display car parks within a ten-minute walk. A lovely, functional community-run resource like Topsham Pool is a labour of love – for those who planned it, fundraised to build it in the 1970s and 1980s and those who look after it now. We will always be grateful to those volunteers and fundraisers, past, present and future for the work they do keeping pools like Topsham open for locals and visitors alike. It is a treat of a pool in a treat of a town.

There is level access to poolside via reception, but access direct from the changing rooms is via the former footbaths, which involves negotiating steps. There are tiled steps, with a handrail, leading into the pool, but no hoist. The changing rooms don't have individual cubicles, and there are some narrow corners and spaces that might make things challenging for disabled swimmers.

There is space to sit out, soaking up the sun, around the pool but it is more likely that a visiting swimmer will head off and explore the town after their swim. This is well worth doing, as it is a pretty and historic place with a good selection of eateries and interesting shops. You could lose yourself for hours in the antique centre down on Topsham Quay.

TUNNELS BEACHES

ENGLAND Devon

Tunnels Beaches
Bath Place, Ilfracombe
Devon
EX34 8AN

- info@tunnelsbeaches.co.uk
- 01271 879882
- tunnelsbeaches.co.uk
- @tunnelsbeaches
- @tunnelsbeaches
- @tunnelsbeaches

- Irregular
- Privately run
- Seasonal
- Unheated
- Saltwater
- Pay and display car park across the road, and on-street parking
- Café on site

Some swims offer a portal through time, and Tunnels Beaches is one of them. They were created to provide the genteel Ilfracombe residents and visitors with a safe place to swim, sheltered from seas that are often wild along this rugged piece of coast. In accordance with the propriety of the day, gender-segregated bathing was the norm, and Tunnels Beaches offered a tidal bathing pool and sheltered beach bathing that kept the womenfolk away from the prying eyes of the men, and vice versa – which was perhaps for the best, given that naked bathing was not uncommon for men at that time.

The clue to the unique feature of this place lies in the name. Having paid your admission money, you access it via a longish tunnel cut into the rock. As you emerge from the gloom of the tunnel you

are immediately struck by the light and landscape. The path winds down to the tidal pool, via further shorter tunnelling, passing various displays of history connected to the site along the way. Bathing is no longer segregated, and this is now a marvellously safe space for family bathing that retains a good deal of the wild about it. There are no facilities to speak of, and being a dab hand at changing under a towel will be a valuable skill to bring to Tunnels Beaches. Wheelchair users will find the paved areas convenient, although some of the inclines may be steeper than would be ideal, but access to the water itself requires navigating a pebbly and uneven beach.

The tidal pool is only just big enough to make it into this book. While it is possible, just, to have a perfectly decent swim if you want it and don't mind a lot of turns, the pool is better suited to larking about. The entry is shallow and sloping, if a little rough and uneven underfoot, as one would expect from what is essentially a giant rock pool dammed by humankind. The seaward side is deep enough for jumping in, which makes it particularly fun for the young and young at heart. As you wallow in the water you can look back to shore and really appreciate the engineering that went into making this facility. The cliff through which you have passed looms above you, mirroring the scale of the vision and ingenuity of those engineers who designed and built it.

Access is predominantly seasonal, but there are some occasional winter openings if a cold dip calls you. Call ahead, or check the website, if you are hoping for a winter visit.

THE ROCK POOL

ENGLAND Devon

The Rock Pool
Westward Ho!, Bideford
Devon
EX39 1LL

- orchardwells@btinternet.com, martin.hom@icloud.com These are email addresses for two of the volunteers who look after The Rock Pool
- 01237 428700
- None
- @TorridgeDC
- Westward Ho! Lido Rock Pool Club

- 22 m x 23 m
- Volunteer run in partnership with the council
- Year round
- Unheated
- Saltwater
- Pay and display parking nearby, the postcode above is for the Westward Ho! Slipway short-stay car park, which is the nearest to the pool.
- Choice of cafés ten minutes' walk away in Westward Ho!

'I learned to swim in that pool' is a refrain we have heard so often in our travels from outdoor pool to outdoor pool, and yet sadly we've heard regularly that the pool in question was demolished in favour of something modern, functional and anodyne. Happily, The Rock Pool very much still exists, and is everything that you'd want a much-cherished pool to be.

With a dramatic coastal setting, where the next bit of land is America as you swim towards the deep end, this is a pool that is only revealed at low tide. We were lucky enough to swim in it at a time when not only had the tide just gone out, but the pool had recently received a good spring clean by the volunteers that look after the pool in a happy relationship with the district council.

You may be wondering, as you read this book, how we've found out so many things about open-air swimming pools and

© Mark Garland

© Mark Garland

how there is so much to say about lidos. There is so much to say in part because every single pool is different and has an operating model that differs from location to location. A swim in an open-air pool is essentially a collection of distinct experiences, just one of which is exercise, and we like to talk to the curators who work hard to make these experiences possible. So if there's an opportunity for a bit of lido chat we always take it, and relish it. We never fail to enjoy the conversation; we hear about the swimmers of all ages who use the pool year round, the positive effect swimming has on their bodies and souls and how the pool is run and maintained. Westward Ho! sea pool is one of those where a good lido chat with one of the volunteers enhanced the swim. It was nice to pass the time hearing about how the pool is cared for as, while this pool is basic and offers no facilities such as changing rooms or toilets, it requires work to keep it free of debris and to keep the paintwork fresh.

This is a lovely pool, of a regular, almost square shape, with graduated steps at the shallow end. Although the deep end is only 1.2 metres deep the pool is long enough to get a good set of strokes across, as locals do daily all year round. The temperature of this unsupervised pool varies from take-your-breath-away brisk to pleasantly refreshing, depending on the time of year. The salty water is refreshed with every tide, and that makes this an authentic, almost wild, swim. You feel that every child who has learned to swim here has also had the pleasure of immersing themselves in both the water and the fun that a seaside open-air pool offers.

Westward Ho! itself is also a delight, with a number of reasonably priced pay and display car parks in the centre of town and a very gentle stroll along the promenade to the pool, shops, cafés and places to have an ice cream. There are no facilities at all at the pool, but the free toilets next to the Co-op have enough space to get changed in. Best to bring a cover-up and some footwear to access this pool, however. You will find it opposite the brightly coloured beach huts and across a small, stony part of the beach, and it is only visible, and swimmable, at low tide. Because of this visitors with restricted mobility will find it challenging to reach.

SHAFTESBURY OASIS SWIMMING POOL

ENGLAND Dorset

Shaftesbury Oasis Swimming Pool
Barton Hill, Shaftesbury
Dorset
SP7 8DQ

- info@shaftesbury-oasis.co.uk
- 01747 853181
- shaftesbury-oasis.com
- @shaftesburyoasis
- @shaftesburyoasisswimmingpool

- 23 m x 9 m
- Council run, in partnership with volunteers
- Seasonal
- Heated
- Freshwater
- Parking available on site
- Snack kiosk

Shaftesbury Oasis is a hidden treasure. It isn't easy to find. If you're going by car your satnav will take you right to the site, but you won't be able to see it at all and you'll be scratching your head and cursing modern technology. Look out for an open quadrangle of what look like almshouses on Barton Hill. You may well need to carry on and park elsewhere in the town and walk back, if you are not lucky enough to find space on Barton Hill itself.

To the left of the quadrangle are some iron gates. The word 'pool' is set into them but when they stand open that isn't immediately apparent, although there is a sign on the wall next to them that you should by now have spotted. Pass through the gates, into what looks like an unpromising alley. By now you will hear the familiar lido soundscape. The entrance is plain and unassuming, and will lie on your left as you reach the end of the alley.

The pool is completely enclosed by high walls, and it is impossible to see it until you are right inside. It's not hard to appreciate why it is ideal for the occasional skinny-dipping sessions that are run here. The majority of the time, however, the dress code is very much as usual. There are a number of small group changing rooms, and

the lockers are poolside so if you want to lock your kit away you'll need to take it with you as you leave the changing rooms. There is only a tiny amount of seating space, not readily accessible from poolside, and the focus here is very much on the pool itself. It is an unusual length, which will be worth bearing in mind if you record your distance. You may find distance impractical, depending when you go, as there is a fine selection of floats available that are very popular with children. This can lend a cheerfully chaotic air that isn't necessarily conducive to racking up the miles.

Cheerful is, perhaps, the word that best defines this pool, not least as a result of the colourful murals that brighten up what would otherwise be fairly dull brick surrounds. The changing areas are a series of small rooms with no individual cubicles, and wheelchair users will find space very tight when manoeuvring through doors and around corners. Access is level, but there are no hoist or sloping steps into the pool itself.

BRIGHTLINGSEA OPEN AIR SWIMMING POOL

ENGLAND Essex

Brightlingsea Open Air Swimming Pool
Promenade Way, Brightlingsea, Colchester
Essex
CO7 0HH

- brightlingsealido@gmail.com
- 01206 303067
- brightlingsealido.org
- @BrightLido
- @brightlido
- @brightlingsealido

- 60 m x 25 m
- Volunteer run
- Seasonal
- Unheated
- Freshwater
- Parking available on site
- Snack kiosk

Brightlingsea is the latest in an increasingly long line of pools that have been saved for the community, by the community. Previously run by Tendring Council, the pool has recently been taken into community stewardship in conjunction with the town council. There is every reason to see this as the start of a bright new period in Brightlingsea's future, and a very welcome development in the life of this irregularly shaped, unheated wonder nestled into the seafront. As you arrive you'll be greeted by a wall mural that professes 'many hands make lido work', perfectly summing up the community efforts that have gone into rescuing this historic facility.

The main tank is vast, with steps into the paddling-pool-depth shallow end. The water deepens gradually, until finally your feet leave the bottom and you're floating. Take some time to look around this bright blue haven; the colours are more reminiscent of a Greek island than the Essex foreshore. The pool is unheated, but warms nicely in the sun, and the separate paddling pool is even warmer. Sunbathing terraces make the most of this suntrap of a site. There are snacks and refreshments available from the kiosk, and this pool would make a good lido road trip with Beccles and Woodup Pool at Tollesbury.

There has been recent improvement to disabled access, with the installation of dedicated changing facilities and ramps to give access to poolside. There are also plans to improve access to the pool itself. As this is work in progress, and subject to change, it is recommended that you call ahead to determine whether your needs can be met.

KINGS OAK HOTEL

ENGLAND Essex

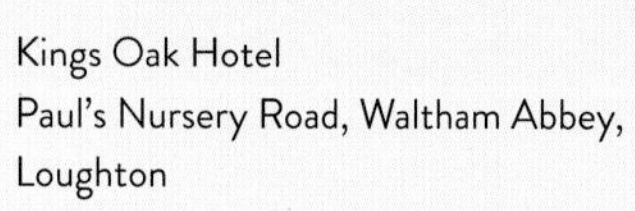

Kings Oak Hotel
Paul's Nursery Road, Waltham Abbey,
Loughton
Essex
IG10 4AE

- info@kingsoakhotel.com
- 020 8508 5000
- kingsoakhotel.com
- @kingsoakhotel
- facebook.com/kingsoakhotel
- @kingsoakeppingforest

- 33 m x 10 m
- Privately run
- Seasonal
- Unheated
- Freshwater
- Free parking available on site
- On-site pub and café

Depending on your age or proclivity for old Hollywood movies, a visit to the open-air pool at the Kings Oak in Epping Forest has the capacity to make you feel like Tracy Lord or Dexter Haven from *High Society*. This is the kind of glorious Art Deco open-air pool that belongs in a movie or on the grounds of a wealthy home, and has also featured in that more local and modern offering, *The Only Way Is Essex*.

It is a truly glorious 33-metre long, deep, blue, unheated pool with a fountain at one end, a white-painted surround and a plethora of sunbeds and loungers on which to while away the day. You might want to plan to spend the whole day here, as this is not a cheap swim. As this was one of the last pools to be swum in, for the purposes of researching this book, it was quite momentous. To reflect on

the journey drawing to a close, while savouring the luxury, felt very special.

The pool is part of a hotel that offers a wedding venue, corporate event space, pub and park café, and is in the centre of Epping Forest near to the visitors' centre, a short drive away from Junction 26 of the M25. It is only open to the public on the afternoons of sunny days when the Kings Oak is not hosting a wedding or other party, so it is *essential* that you call ahead to check opening times and prices for you (and your party).

The staff are friendly on the phone and equally friendly and efficient once you arrive. Before you know it you'll be diving in. While the pool is glorious, particularly if you enjoy the opportunity to be the only one swimming in it, the two individual male and female changing huts-cum-toilets feel a bit rudimentary and you will need to take your own towel. With the expense of the swim, you might think a towel is included; it isn't.

Make no mistake, this is a glorious refreshing swim on a hot day. But this is not your average open-air swimming pool and careful planning to drive here on a day when it is publicly open is required; it isn't a 'turn up and swim on a whim' sort of place. There are two good places for post-swim eats and drinks – the pub with a beer garden that forms the majority of the Kings Oak Hotel serves hot food, and the kiosk-style café with picnic benches outside that has an extensive menu.

Twitter provided us with the phrase 'millionaire's swim' to describe those days when you have a perfect swim and enjoy being alone in the pool, and this pool was worth saving, until the research for the book was drawing to a close, to indulge in that very type of swim.

WOODUP POOL

ENGLAND Essex

Woodup Pool, Tollesbury
Woodrolfe Road, Tollesbury, Maldon
Essex
CM9 8SE

- tollesburypc@btinternet.com
- 01621 869039
- essexinfo.net/tollesbury-parish-council/woodup-pool
- @woodupool

- Approximately 100 m x 75 m
- Council run
- Seasonal
- Unheated
- Saltwater
- No parking on site, nearest car park a ten-minute walk away along Woodrolfe Road
- None available

Woodup Pool is a rare treat – not least because it is free to swim in. It's a semi-natural open-air pool, with man-made boundaries on three sides and a small beach area on the fourth. Filled with saltwater, it is flushed through once every ten days or so, at high tide, which keeps the water clear and cool. The margin of the pool is home to plant life, and at the centre it is plenty deep enough for a decent swim. If you were minded to make circuits around the red-and-white pole markers you'd probably have a loop of around 200 metres at your disposal.

If you're the kind of swimmer who prefers to swim without purpose, to bob and float while enjoying the view, there will be much to keep you interested here. The pool sits alongside a working marina and boatyard, serving the saltings – a traditional Essex mud-berth

type of mooring. A forest of masts surrounds the pool, and the traditional boats both ashore and afloat are a slice of history that you'll breathe in with every lungful of good, clean salt air.

The beach area is popular with families, and there are picnic tables and some brick-built barbecue facilities open to all to use. Sometimes an ice-cream seller is stationed near the beach area, and there is a café in the former sail loft buildings across the road. This is a pool where one could easily spend a whole day, alternating dipping in and out of the water with retiring ashore with a good book and a flask of tea. Children will love it here, as it will feel like an adventurous swim, and it is a safe place for them to splash about with inflatables. Parents will want to note the lack of lifeguards, however, and read the safety information signage around the pool.

Less mobile swimmers may find this pool challenging, as accessing it involves crossing some rough, sloping ground and sand. There are some steps with handrails giving access to the water at various points, but that may involve entering into some of the weed and plant life on the margins, which is not to everybody's taste. There are no toilet facilities.

BATHURST OPEN AIR POOL

ENGLAND Gloucestershire

Bathurst Open Air Pool
High Street, Bream, Lydney
Gloucestershire
GL15 5DY

mail@bathurstpool.co.uk
01594 842625
bathurstpool.co.uk
@BathurstPool
@BathurstPool

- 33 m x 17 m
- Volunteer run
- Seasonal
- Unheated
- Freshwater
- Free parking available on site
- Snack kiosk

Lydney is a charming little Forest of Dean town that, curiously, if coming from the south or east you will pass through Wales briefly to reach. This can be a little confusing, but stick with it. If driving, and you probably will be as this pool is not easily accessible via public transport, your satnav will take you right to the door, but the entrance off the main road is understated and you'll need to look carefully to spot the signage.

The car park is essentially a field, and the perimeter wall reveals little of what is on offer inside aside from the painted mural that livens up the breeze-block construction. The painting is what links inside and outside. The volunteers who run this pool have created a colourful and vibrant thing of beauty from the unpromising blank canvas.

The pool itself is very much the star, large and deeply blue with a waterfall running gently into the shallow end. The pool is heated, but not much, so your swim will feel crisp and cool on a hot day and welcomingly warm in cooler weather – the best of both worlds.

Every square inch of the poolside area is dressed in finery. The murals on the walls are funny, sweet, bright and cheerful. The colourful changing-cubicle doors are a sight to warm the heart of any lido-nostalgia lover. There are Mediterranean-coloured sails acting as sunshades over the picnic tables, and a soft floor covering to give comfort to bare feet. The kiosk is equally jolly, and well stocked.

There are little in the way of visual clues to give away the age of this facility, but a plaque on the wall on the opposite side of the pool to the sunshades reveals that it was established as a gift of benevolence to the community in 1920. A gift that has undoubtedly kept on giving. More of the history is hidden away, including the original filter that remains the powerhouse of the plant system.

This pool will require you to go out of your way to visit – but you will come away feeling as though you have packed a holiday into just a few hours.

If you succeed in securing a parking space outside the pool you will find level, if a bit bumpy, access to the entrance, and the poolside beyond is also level. Access to the pool is via ladders, and there is no hoist.

CIRENCESTER OPEN AIR SWIMMING POOL

ENGLAND Gloucestershire

Cirencester Open Air Swimming Pool
Cecily Hill, Cirencester
Gloucestershire
GL7 2EF

- secretary@cirenopenair.co.uk
- 01285 653947
- cirenopenair.co.uk
- @COASP1869
- @CirencesterOpenAirSwimmingPool
- @cirenopenair

- 28 m x 14 m
- Volunteer run
- Seasonal
- Heated
- Freshwater
- Council-run car parks at Sheep Street and the Old Station, Tetbury Road
- Snack kiosk

There are some pools that leave a swimmer seriously contemplating moving house just to live nearby. Cirencester will easily make that shortlist for many swimmers. The town itself is windingly, historically beautiful. A relatively short walk to the pool is inevitable, whether you arrive in town by car or public transport, but it will be worth lengthening that walk to take in a little of the town if you can.

The sign diverting you off the road and down a path to the pool has an ornate, antique style that is completely in keeping with the surroundings, and you'll cross

a small footbridge to the pool entrance. Once inside the pool area, that bridge will feel like a drawbridge, as the view beyond the pool is dominated by castellated stone former barracks that look like a castle fit for a king.

The buildings surrounding the pool are of a very different style, with a plain but useful and well-stocked kiosk at the far end and a very modern changing block and plant room near the gate. Those changing facilities are definitely a boon on a cool day, but the showers are coin operated so take some small change into the shower with you alongside your shampoo and towel. If you're interested in the machinery that cleans and maintains the water this is one of the few pools where you can peep through glass into the plant room. (Portishead and Bourne are other must-visit destinations for plant-room window gazers.)

Set in very spacious paved grounds, with pretty planting and wooden benches whose plaques speak to the importance of this place to members of

this community, the two heated pools are both an excellent size. The main pool has a slide, and there is usually a lane in for the more purposeful swimmers. The toddler pool is often well stocked with inflatable toys and floats. Picnics are welcome, and this is a pool where you could easily lose yourself for hours, enjoying the water, the view and the friendly community atmosphere that comes as much from the swimmers as it does from the volunteers. It's easy to strike up a conversation here, if you are so inclined, and if you do you'll hear memories and stories that make it clear that this pool is tightly knit into the lives of those that love it.

The walk required to reach the pool contributes to its secluded feel, but swimmers with reduced mobility will need to bear that in mind. Once inside the changing rooms are readily accessible. Access to the pool is via ladders (or the slide!) and there is no hoist.

NORTHLEACH SWIMMING POOL

ENGLAND Gloucestershire

Northleach Swimming Pool
Northleach Primary School, Mill End,
Northleach, Cheltenham
Gloucestershire
GL54 3HJ

- fonspool@gmail.com
- None
- none
- @northleachpool

- 15 m x 4 m
- Volunteer run
- Seasonal
- Heated
- Freshwater
- Small car park outside school
- None available

Northleach hovers on the margins of being big enough to qualify for a place in this book. It is truly dinky, but size does not always matter.

It will matter to you if you want to bash out some mileage, but this is not a pool for that. In many ways, it is not really a pool for swimmers at all, given that the 'deep' end is only waist deep for an average-sized adult and the shallow end much shallower. Smaller lido fans, however, will feel happy and secure in a heated pool that is tailor made for the proportions of childhood. And the adults accompanying those small swimmers can while away a happy hour wading, splashing or sitting on the edge with feet dangling into the water. Sometimes it does us all good to be in touch with our inner child.

Northleach is likely to appeal to committed lido hunters, or those passing through or living in the area with small children. Please note that we refer to passing a happy hour with good reason – the pool predominantly serves the primary school that it sits behind; from the car park you access the pool via what looks like a small farm track running to the left of the school. It is, therefore, only open to the public for about an hour a day after school ends in the second half of the summer term. Contact Friends of Northleach Swimming Pool direct to check weekend and holiday opening hours. There are no airs and graces at Northleach, with no facilities to speak of. Be prepared to change under a towel and buy your snacks in the village – a village that is as achingly beautiful as you'd expect from the Cotswolds.

SANDFORD PARKS LIDO

ENGLAND Gloucestershire

Sandford Parks Lido
Keynsham Road, Cheltenham
Gloucestershire
GL53 7PU

- swim@sandfordparkslido.org.uk
- 01242 524430
- sandfordparkslido.org.uk
- @lidocheltenham
- @sandfordparkslido
- @sandfordparkslido

- 50 m x 20 m
- Volunteer run
- Seasonal
- Heated
- Freshwater
- Pay and display car park on site
- On-site café

Regency Cheltenham, as you might imagine, is home to a lot of impressive buildings. The lido stands shoulder to shoulder with them all being, as it is, one of the grand old ladies of the remaining UK lidos. Set against some of those long-lost behemoths, such as the Morecambe Super Swimming Stadium, Portobello or Larkswood, it would probably look quite understated given the elegant simplicity of its architecture.

The huge site is dominated by two period crescent buildings. The first housing the entryway, complete with iron turnstiles and original outdoor changing cubicles. The former basket stores have since been converted into modern, heated indoor changing facilities at the end of each arm of the crescents – men to the left and women to the right as you enter.

The second crescent, visible beyond the classic wedding-cake fountain that dominates your early view of the place, houses a café and shady terracing with seating.

The crescents bookend the site, and in between lies an enormous tank that has been restored to its original period

finish, complete with graciously curved ceramic scum channels that were specially made for the refurbishment. This feature has fallen out of fashion, with the advent of modern skimmer systems and deck-level pools; that's a great shame because they are perfectly designed for holding on to as you pause in your swim. Look out for the ceramic depth markers, a pleasing period feature, among many retained during the refurbishment of the main pool and surrounding areas in 2006/2007.

There is also a second smaller pool for younger or less confident swimmers, complete with a small slide to mirror the enormous steel slide that still graces the main tank. Younger visitors will also appreciate the small play area.

The whole site is grassy, and pleasant for a day-long outing. It is an ideal location for special events, and the outdoor concert and theatre programme for the summer season is well worth a look if you want an excuse to visit with a non-swimming friend or family member.

Car parking is immediately outside the pool and, once inside, only the café requires navigating steps to enter. There is a wide, shallow flight of steps with good handrails offering access down into the shallow end. These factors combine to make Sandford Parks perform well in the accessibility stakes – only a hoist and dedicated disabled shower or wet-room would improve matters.

© Roger Taylor

STRATFORD PARK LIDO

ENGLAND Gloucestershire

Stratford Park Lido
Stratford Road, Stroud
Gloucestershire
GL5 4AF

stratfordparkinfo@everyoneactive.com
01453 766771
everyoneactive.com/centre/stratford-park-leisure-centre
@eaStratfordPark
@eaStratfordPark

50 m x 20 m
Corporately operated on behalf of the council
Seasonal
Unheated
Freshwater
Parking available on site
On-site café

This pool is an unexpected, and almost criminally under-utilised, period gem in the heart of Stroud. While the corporate operator runs other lidos with pride and passion, including Tinside, that pride and passion doesn't seem to have trickled down to Stratford Park, where one gets the impression that the outdoor pool is run as an inconvenient afterthought to the modern leisure centre next door.

We get that rare bit of negativity out of the way up front, because we want you to know that when you visit Stratford you will have a truly excellent swim despite all that.

You might find, when you arrive, that the staff at the ticket desk tell you the pool is freezing, and remind you that they might inexplicably close it if it starts to rain. You might feel a bit disappointed when you realise that the period-looking entranceway contains a slightly shabby, and not always spotlessly clean, communal changing area that does no justice at all to the building itself, or what lies behind.

But then you will glimpse the pool, and you will forget

about all of that. At 50 metres long it is inspiring in scale, as are the listed original diving platforms that really are the knock-out feature of this pool. They are no longer in use, a sadly common scenario that arises from a combination of changing health and safety legislation and the difficulty of managing the risks of diving alongside a general swimming session. The platforms rise on elliptical legs in homage to the much larger, similarly designed platforms that once towered over the now defunct Tropicana in Weston-super-Mare. The blue of the water reflects off the white undersides of the platforms themselves, to mercurial effect.

The water is not heated, it is true, but it is far from freezing. The diving platforms have given this pool an unusual underwater profile, such that it has two shallow ends and a shallow side. This makes it ideal for swimmers who like to be within their depth, and the shallow parts of the pool do warm readily in the sun. The diving-well area is often not open for swimming, and is roped off in what appears to a frustrating effort to reduce staff costs.

The grounds around the pool are a combination of paved terracing and grass; they are perfect for picnicking and lounging after your swim, but might present some challenges for wheelchair users, as would access to the water in the absence of a hoist.

Outdoor 50-metre pools are a thing of increasing rarity, and ones that lie in spacious green grounds, with iconic listed diving platforms and the potential to run some very special events in those grounds, are much in a minority. People can, will and should travel to swim here, but we fervently hope that the operator of this pool comes to recognise the heritage and potential that is Stratford Park. We don't doubt that at present this pool doesn't generate enough income to make it seem like an attractive proposition compared to its indoor neighbour. But if properly run all that could change.

Please show the operator how much this pool matters by visiting it and passing on some of your enthusiasm; you will love your swim here.

WOTTON POOL

ENGLAND Gloucestershire

Wotton Pool
Symn Lane, Wotton-under-Edge
Gloucestershire
GL12 7BD

- info@wottonpool.co.uk
- 01453 842086
- wottonpool.co.uk
- @WottonPool
- @WottonPool

- 18 m x 6 m
- Volunteer run
- Seasonal
- Heated
- Freshwater
- On-street parking outside and car park 100 m away
- None available

Wotton is one of just a handful of pools we've included in *The Lido Guide* that is only an open-air pool on *some* days. Its retractable roof makes it very versatile – a village swimming pool that can be used in all weathers during the season and particularly enjoyed on warm and sunny days when the roof is open. The semicircular glass domes that cover the pool concertina into each other when the weather is nice, giving some space to sit around the pool but mainly to enjoy the experience of swimming in the open air.

It is a standard 18-metre, three-lane swimming pool with open-plan male and female changing rooms in the main entrance block. We are not able to give up-to-date disability access information for this pool, as on the last occasion we arrived to swim it was unexpectedly closed and Wotton Pool has not replied to our enquiries about accessibility. If you are travelling any distance to visit it would be wise to call ahead and check whether your needs can be met.

The water is gently heated by solar panels. Open April to September, this pool is run as a community enterprise by volunteers from within the village for the people of the village, although visitors are welcome. It is worth a detour from the M5 to swim here and support community swimming.

The centre of Wotton offers car parking, shops, cafés and pubs, which is useful as there is no catering available on site at the pool.

PLEASE DO NOT
ENTER WATER UNTIL
A LIFE GUARD OR

ALDERSHOT LIDO

ENGLAND Hampshire

Aldershot Lido
Guildford Road, Aldershot
Hampshire
GU12 4BP

- enquiries@aldershotpoolscomplex.co.uk
- 01252 323482
- aldershotlido.co.uk
- @aldershotpools
- @aldershotlidoofficial
- @aldershotlido

- Irregular
- Council run
- Seasonal
- Unheated
- Freshwater
- Free parking available on site
- Snack kiosk

That the garrison town of Aldershot is home to one of the larger, and more historic, of the UK's lidos is news to a lot of people. The site doesn't announce itself, and the approach through residential streets feels curiously out of kilter with what you will find at the end of your journey.

The dominant feature of Aldershot Lido are the water slides that tower over the site in bold primary colours, but everything about Aldershot is on an impressive scale. The site is huge and grassy, and the pool itself is split into four distinct areas.

There is a semicircular sloping entry with the traditional lido fountain at its centre. This is perfect for children and toe dippers, and adults with very small children can sit in the shallows, keeping their little ones at hand. This gives way to a

roped-off zone set up to protect general swimmers from being landed on by a self-propelled swimming missile being fired from the bottom of the slides.

The shallow hemisphere gradually gives way to deeper water, which is helpful for access. That develops into part of the tank that has straight, parallel sides. This is the lane-swimming area, and it is perfectly suited to the task. Beyond that lies a deep diving well with a diving platform still in place above.

On quieter days you might find that not all parts of the lido are open. This pool is challenging and labour intensive to supervise given its unusual shape and varying depths. However, when we have visited we've found the staff to be responsive to requests from swimmers to open any closed parts, even if only for a defined period of time.

The water is unheated, so it can feel cool on chilly days, but there are indoor changing rooms, hot showers, hot chocolate and snacks available from the kiosk afterwards and the site lends itself to impromptu running races around the trees to warm up any children who might shiver on cooler days. This pool looks like, and is, the archetypal hot-weather pool, but please don't let less than perfect weather put you off. The slide fanatics among you will get a much bigger bang for your buck on a grey day, as you won't have to queue.

Aldershot has a good range of disability access provision, including a hoist and dedicated changing facilities. The slides, however, feature stairs to be climbed and that cannot be avoided.

HILSEA LIDO

ENGLAND Hampshire

Hilsea Lido
London Road, Hilsea, Portsmouth
Hampshire
PO2 9RP

info@hilsea-lido.org.uk
07903 823347
hilsea-lido.org.uk
@HilseaLido
@hilsealido
@hilsealido

67 m x 18 m
Independent trust
Seasonal
Unheated
Freshwater
Parking available on site
On-site café

Hilsea Lido is the epitome of what *The Lido Guide* is about. It is about finding a bright, shining, glittery diamond of a pool that you didn't know existed and having a great swim there. This is a community pool nestled below the M27, on the A3 near Portsmouth, run by a small but dedicated band of volunteers who have not only saved the historic Art Deco pool but who tirelessly run it for locals and visitors alike and raise money to restore it. It is truly a pool for the people.

There is so much to say about this pool, which rarely features in the 'Top 10 Outdoor Swim' type articles we are so familiar with. It is a big, big, pool. It is full of unheated freshwater. It has a diving board in the centre of the pool that young and old jump from. Like Guildford Lido and Stratford Park, this pool is deepest in the middle, at 4.5 metres, with two shallow ends at either end of the pool. It is a long swim at 67 metres from end to end.

The gate is a bright and cheerful welcome to a pool that occupies the central space of this large site. There are great swathes of places to sit around the pool, and although there is no getting away from the fact that these are largely concreted areas rather than grassy banks, they still make a perfect place from which to enjoy your picnic. You are free to bring in your own food and soft drinks, and there are refreshments to buy on site from the tea room, the Blue Lagoon.

At the time of writing the large pool buildings still required some restoration to maximise their potential, and fundraising was underway for that. For now, they enclose large changing rooms, toilets and showers. There are wide doorways, and level access to the site but no hoist.

Free car parking on site enhances a visit to Hilsea Lido, perhaps leaving you with some spare change to contribute towards the fundraising to restore this lido to its full and former glory.

LYMINGTON SEA WATER BATHS

ENGLAND Hampshire

Lymington Sea Water Baths
Bath Road, Lymington
Hampshire
SO41 3SE

- info@lymingtonseawaterbaths.org.uk
- 01590 678882
- lymingtonseawaterbaths.org.uk
- @LymingtonSWB
- @lymingtonseawaterbaths

- 110 m x 50 m
- Privately run
- Seasonal
- Unheated
- Saltwater
- Bath Road council car park located thirty seconds away
- Snack kiosk

Lido nomenclature is a tricky business that extends well beyond the thorny issue of pronunciation; do you say ly-doh or lee-doh? There are some pools that resolutely refuse to call themselves a lido. They shy away from the word precisely because of its exotic otherness. The users of these pools don't see them as exotic, or other. They see themselves as everyday swimmers.

In southern parts of the UK the most common alternative is 'open-air pool' or 'outdoor pool'. The further north one travels, while still remaining south of Hadrian's Wall, it is more likely you'll be told that the word you are looking for is 'baths' – a nod to the utilitarian roots of public swimming in baths and washhouses.

Lymington is, therefore, something of an anomaly in name. And what a glorious anomaly it is. The pool, full of pumped and filtered seawater, is enormous, and very clever use of the space is made to provide a sizeable swimming area, a huge inflatable assault course, zorbing, stand-up paddle boarding and a safe space for younger swimmers. The jetty on the far side of the pool is perfect for jumping off; a perennial pleasure. This pool is ideal for group visits, as between the waterborne activities, sunloungers and excellent ice cream available from the kiosk, there is something to please every member of the party. Given all that is on offer the admission price is very reasonable, and you pay only for the activities you want to do; a thoroughly decent and sensible approach.

The bottom of the pool is covered in some sort of pea shingle, which is a surprise if you're not expecting it. If you think you won't like the way that feels, then you might want to consider taking some beach shoes to wear in the water, but it isn't at all sharp or painful underfoot. There isn't any view to speak of from this pool, as it sits in a dip, but that has the advantage of providing a great deal of shelter from the sea breeze. The view outside the pool is well worth pausing to drink in as you approach, however – a bucolic and classically English estuarine sight.

Some walking, on a level tarmac-covered surface, is required to reach this pool. The tank is quite accessible, with steps featuring handrails as well as the shallow area. There is no hoist, however, and wheelchair users might find the changing rooms a bit tight on space.

PETERSFIELD OPEN AIR POOL

ENGLAND Hampshire

Petersfield Open Air Pool
Heath Road, Petersfield
Hampshire
GU31 4DZ

- info@petersfieldpool.org
- 01730 265143
- petersfieldpool.org
- @ptrsfldpoolopen
- Petersfield Open Air Swimming Pool
- @petersfieldopenairpool

- 25 m x 10 m
- Volunteer run
- Seasonal
- Heated
- Freshwater
- Parking available in Festival Hall car park
- Snack kiosk

This pool sits in a car park in the middle of town. And while that undoubtedly makes it ideal for lido road trippers, it doesn't lend much charm to the exterior, although a reliably appealing period brick façade does its best to stand up against that.

Inside, however, is a very different story, and charm abounds. The pool itself is a solidly useful 25-metre tank full of heated water, with a diving board still in place; that alone is a rare treat and we're pleased to say that use of it is permitted at some sessions. But the real charm surrounds the pool. There are traditional poolside changing cubicles with brightly coloured doors, as well as some indoor facilities. The site is immaculately and carefully maintained in every respect, with flowers dotted around to add additional splashes of colour.

The paved terracing is a lovely place to while away some time post-swim, with a pergola lending some shade on hot days. During the heated season there is a nice mix of sessions, offering swimmers a lot of choice. In winter, when the pool runs unheated swimming at weekends, there is a fire pit over which to warm tingling fingers.

The real heat that radiates from Petersfield, however, comes from the people who run the pool.

They love this place, and rightly so. It feels like a community hub that embraces all comers. Given Petersfield's location this is a pool that lends itself to a side visit while you're en route to and from any number of places. Well worth having up your sleeve to break a journey, or for an afternoon out in its own right.

There is ramped access into the site, and the pool surrounds are level and smooth. The poolside changing cubicles and showers/toilets will be a tight squeeze for wheelchair users, however, and the tank is accessed via ladders.

HEMEL HEMPSTEAD OUTDOOR POOL

ENGLAND Hertfordshire

Hemel Hempstead Outdoor Pool
Hemel Hempstead Sportspace, Park Road,
Hemel Hempstead
Hertfordshire
HP1 1JS

- hempsteadinfo@everyoneactive.com
- 01442 507100
- everyoneactive.com/centre/hemel-hempstead-leisure-centre
- @HemelLeisure
- @HemelLeisure

- 25 m x 10 m
- Corporately run on behalf of the council
- Seasonal
- Heated
- Freshwater
- Parking available on site
- On-site café

You would think that in a book about around 130 open-air UK pools that we'd be struggling for something to say about each one. Not so. First and foremost we are, of course, looking for a great swim but aside from that there are always other things that attract our attention and linger in the memory.

So, what is there that's memorable about the open-air pool in Hemel Hempstead? Run by a leisure company under contract to the council, this pool is part of a complex (with parking on site, within walking distance from the centre of town and from the station) which houses an indoor pool, a diving pool, gym and sports/leisure courses. It also sells swimming and sports essentials and has an on-site café. The grassy-verge-flanked pool is accessed through a familiar changing village, which is fully disabled accessible, and via a short walk alongside the indoor pools.

These things don't make the 25-metre outdoor pool any

different from other similarly efficient leisure centre set-ups. However, most pools follow a set-up where the shallow part of the pool is at one end, leading to the deep end either in the middle, like Hilsea, Stratford Park and Guildford, or at one end. At Hemel Hempstead, as at Saltdean, the deep end runs the entire length of one side of the pool, while the shallow end runs the entire length of the graduated stepped entry side of this rectangular pool. It is a slightly unfamilar setup, but it has distinct advantages in that it allows for younger and more experienced swimmers to swim lengths alongside each other in their own relevant depths (although the serious swimmers naturally tend to make a claim on the deepest side of the pool first). The set-up also allows for easy access via the steps, which will be a bonus for swimmers with restricted mobility although there is no hoist.

HITCHIN SWIMMING CENTRE

ENGLAND Hertfordshire

Hitchin Swimming Centre
Fishponds Road, Hitchin
Hertfordshire
SG5 1HA

- enquiries.hitchin@sll.co.uk
- 01462 441646
- sll.co.uk/enterprise/Hitchin_Swimming
- @ArchersGym
- @HitchinSwimmingCentre

- 50 m x 20 m
- Corporately run on behalf of the council
- Seasonal
- Heated
- Freshwater
- Parking available on site
- On-site café

Hitchin is a wonderful example of how modern leisure and swimming facilities can be built around a fine example of a late-1930s lido. The original building still stands, with changing areas and a function room, but access to the pool is now via the more modern building on the other side of the pool. That building forms a clever bridge between the history of the lido and the modernity of the indoor pool and leisure centre.

There are changing facilities inside the leisure centre that offer every modern convenience, including good disabled access. Lido swimmers can choose to use these, or the original, less glamorous and less accessible, 1930s changing facilities in the old building. The modern building also houses a café that serves the lido.

While the modern facilities are open all year, the lido is seasonal. The main tank is 50 metres long, heated and offers somewhat narrow sloping steps with a handrail into the shallow end. There are no hoist facilities. There is also a smaller paddling pool, and both pools are surrounded by paved and grassed sunbathing areas complete with sunloungers – free to use for early birds who arrive in time to stake a claim with a towel. The size of the site means that a lot of people can be admitted, which will likely make this a pool that doesn't suffer from hot-day queues to quite the extent that some other pools do. It is possible to make your way around the terraces without encountering steps, thanks to clever use of ramps – the ramp from the leisure-centre changing areas is quite steep, however.

Swimming at Hitchin feels like a holiday in time as well as space. The 1930s heritage of this place is well preserved, and there is an air of friendly contentment about the place. It will tell you something about how enjoyable a swim here is to know that when we swam here, we intended to stay an hour or so, but stayed for five hours and were still reluctant to leave.

LETCHWORTH OUTDOOR POOL

ENGLAND Hertfordshire

Letchworth Outdoor Pool
Norton Common, Icknield Way, Letchworth
Hertfordshire
SG6 4UF

- None
- 01462 684673
- sll.co.uk/enterprise/LetchworthOutdoorPool
- @LGC_OutdoorPool
- @LetchworthOutdoorPool

- 50 m x 20 m
- Corporately run on behalf of the council
- Seasonal
- Heated
- Freshwater
- Parking available on site
- On-site café

When Letchworth Garden City was planned and built as one of the world's first 'new towns' at the turn of the twentieth century, it was with foresight that those plans and buildings included an open-air swimming pool. When so many other towns and cities across the UK have closed, demolished and filled in their open-air pools, you have to be grateful that someone kept Letchworth Outdoor Pool from meeting the fate of so many of those built at the same time.

This heated 50-metre pool is one that you might not be aware of as you zip up and down the A1(M), and yet it would be perfect as part of a lido road trip taking in the open-air pools of Hitchin, Cambridge and Ware.

Swimming in a 50-metre pool is different to swimming in a 25-metre pool in many ways, only one of which is the obvious fact that it is twice as long. A

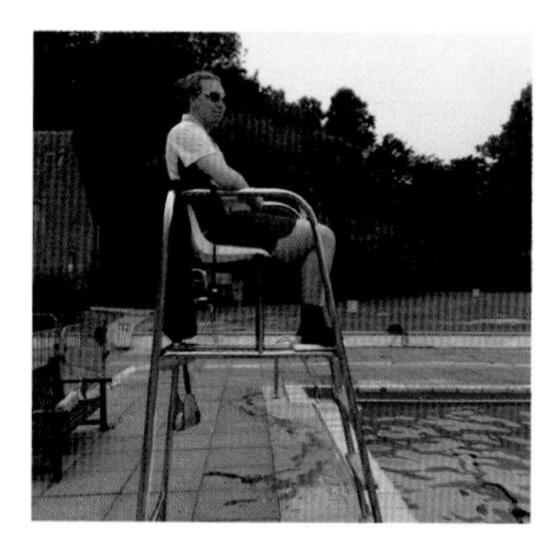

swim at Letchworth, as at other large pools, really allows you a good stretch of a swim, the opportunity to focus on getting a regular rhythm going and to do a tumble turn in the deep end, pushing off into a large expanse of blue for your next lap. Of course, that uninterrupted bliss may not be possible on a warm day when the pool is busy with a wide range of ages. But at an early morning swim session, or on an overcast or drizzly day, a long and relatively empty swimming pool facilitates that workout. Rounding the whole

thing off with a nod to, or a chat with, your fellow swimmers sets you up perfectly for a cuppa from the on-site café afterwards. Swimmers visiting with families will appreciate the toddler pool, and the grassy surroundings that seem tailor-made for picnics.

Accessibility to the pool at the shallow end is made easier with a set of graduated steps into the 0.75-metre depth as well as the traditional poolside steps, and although there are steps to navigate between reception and the pool, the swimmers we noticed with walking aids were able to navigate entry to the pool using the large, flat steps and handrails. If a hoist is essential to you, please call ahead and check the current position. There is a decent-sized car park alongside the pool, with two hours of free parking available for all.

We can only imagine what the planners had in mind when they built a pool into this new town, but outdoor swimming fits perfectly with the spirit of peaceful cooperation and friendly community that was so important in the early years of new town development.

WARE PRIORY LIDO

ENGLAND Hertfordshire

Ware Priory Lido
Priory Street, Ware
Hertfordshire
SG12 0DE

- sean@waretowncouncil
- 01920 460703
- waretowncouncil.gov.uk/services/priory-lido
- @ware_lido
- Friends of Ware Lido (FOWL)

- 30 m x 11 m
- Council run in partnership with volunteers
- Seasonal
- Heated
- Freshwater
- Some parking on site or pay and display car parks on Priory Street or Burgage Lane
- Snack kiosk

Even before you go to Ware Priory Lido you have a sense that there is something *historic* about it, and although it is less than a hundred years old, it has the feel of being older. Set in the grounds of Ware Priory, which dates back to the fourteenth century, it offers a view of part of the priory as you swim from the shallow end to deep end of this 30-metre heated pool.

There are other visual treats at this lovely pool too – artists have taken the time to draw jaunty swimming-related pictures on the inside of the tank, so when you're underwater you have something to look at other than fellow swimmers in the pool, and there is a good opportunity to have a decent length swim here. There's good family fun to be had in the main pool, which has a decent shallow end for little ones, and there is also a toddler pool.

There is a large grassy bank overlooking part of the priory at one end of the pool, suitable for picnics, and the pool entrance, standard changing rooms and shower buildings at the other. There is dedicated disabled changing facility within the family changing area, and access all around the site is level or ramped. There are sloping steps with a handrail on one side, to gain entry to the water, but no hoist.

It is a sheltered spot, perfect for family or solo swimming and within walking distance of the station in Ware along a high street where there are plenty of places for post-swim coffee, cake and browsing.

0-70
NO JUMPING OVER STEPS

WATERSIDE POOL

ENGLAND Isle of Wight

Waterside Pool
The Esplanade, Ryde
Isle of Wight
PO33 1JA

- enquiries@watersidepool.co.uk
- 01983 563656
- watersidepool.co.uk
- @RydeWaterside
- @RydeWaterside
- @watersidepool_

- 25 m x 10 m
- Charitable trust run, in partnership with the council
- Year round
- Heated
- Freshwater
- On-street parking
- Snack kiosk

Waterside Pool is one of the few pools included in *The Lido Guide* that isn't always a lido – it is a former open-air pool transformed into a year-round heated community swimming pool by the addition of large glass windows along the promenade and lakeside edges of the pool and a retractable roof. It is a light, bright space and, on a warm day, is open to the sky.

The pool has loungers and seats around it that look out over the beach and the Solent, towards Portsmouth. It is within decent walking distance of Ryde Pier Head, and a shorter walk from the Ryde Esplanade station on the Isle of Wight railway, which uses former London Tube trains to transport passengers between the pier head and Sandown. There is parking on site if you travel by car, but it might be cheaper to be a foot passenger on the ferry from Portsmouth if you are visiting from the mainland for the swim alone.

We urge you to call ahead before you set off if you are looking to swim when the roof is open. As we've mentioned in this guide already, there are a wide variety of (sometimes unpredictable) opening hours for open-air pools in the UK and those that are only occasionally open air need extra checking to avoid disappointment before you go.

This is a lovely pool when the roof is open, and even more enjoyable if you can swim when it is dark outside and then warm up with a hot chocolate from the kiosk-style refreshments area adjacent to reception. The changing rooms are well laid out, with plenty of lockers, and this pool is worth a visit not only to swim in the open air but to enjoy the sensation of watching the roof open to reveal the sky beyond it.

Waterside takes accessibility very seriously and any disabled visitor will find their needs well met with dedicated changing areas, extensive wheelchair access and hoists.

We don't have an image of Waterside Pool, so here's some fun from Walpole Bay Tidal Pool.

FAVERSHAM OUTDOOR POOL

ENGLAND Kent

Faversham Outdoor Pool
Leslie Smith Drive, Faversham
Kent
ME13 8PW

- comments@favershampools.com
- 01795 532426
- favershampools.com
- @FavershamPools
- @FavPools
- @favershampools

- 33 m x 12 m
- Corporately run on behalf of the council
- Seasonal
- Heated
- Freshwater
- Neighbouring council-run car park
- On-site café and snack kiosk

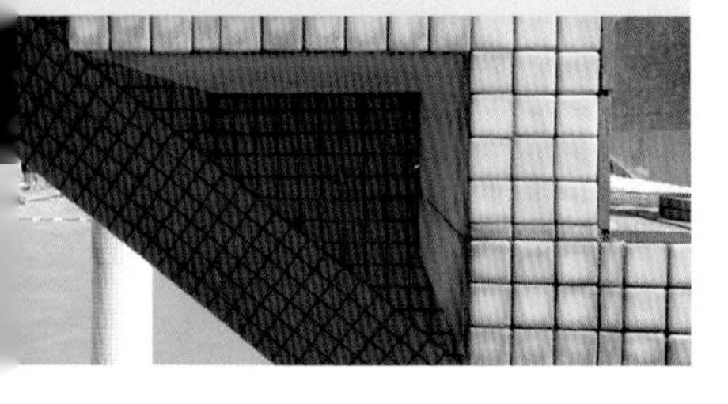

Arriving at the pools, you'll catch a glimpse of the outdoor swimming opportunities and the three (yes, three!) diving boards while queuing at reception to pay. We use the word queuing advisedly, because on warm days this pool is very popular and you could expect to queue for at least an hour. There is a 25-metre indoor pool in this complex but the real attraction for lido lovers obviously lies outside.

This heated pool is a luscious 33 metres long, allowing a really decent swim, and with 1-metre, 3-metre and 5-metre diving boards it allows a really decent dive as well. During public sessions you can expect the deep end to be roped off for significant chunks of the day, so you might want to check by calling ahead if swimming full lengths is what your heart desires. It's hard to begrudge the loss of the deep end, however, as publicly

accessible high diving is a rare thing in the modern world. And there is much pleasure gained from watching the aerial acrobatics as folk try to outdo themselves. If these treats weren't enough on their own, the areas that surround the pool, changing blocks and lockers provide plenty of space to relax and have a picnic. There is a lazy river, which is separate to the pool, that is particularly popular with younger visitors.

The changing rooms are comparatively modern, and have good disabled access. The site is level all around, and there is a hoist giving access to the shallow end of the main pool.

With only ice creams, light snacks and drinks available for sale on site you'll need to look further afield for anything more substantial to complement this lido visit if you haven't brought a picnic. A walk into the town centre of Faversham leads you to the attractive central marketplace and might make you wonder why you've never been there before, as there is lots to see.

THE STRAND POOL

ENGLAND Kent

The Strand Pool

The Strand Leisure Park, Strand Approach Road, Gillingham

Kent

ME7 1TT

- leisure@medway.gov.uk
- 01634 333925
- Council: medway.gov.uk/directory_record/359/the_strand_swimming_pool
  Friends group:www.strandpool.info
- Council: @MedwaySport
  Friends: @strandlido
- Council: @MedwaySportOfficial
  Friends: @strandlidoopenforswimming

- 25 m x 25 m
- Council run, in partnership with volunteers
- Seasonal
- Unheated
- Freshwater
- Parking available on site
- Snack kiosk

The Strand sits on the estuary foreshore of this Medway town, just around an hour out of central London, and nothing about the exterior gives away what lies within. If you come by car you'll park pretty much right outside, and you'll approach the low-slung façade through a park that is very popular with families. You might well be tempted to swing right and stroll along the estuary, avoiding altogether the unremarkable-looking buildings that front the pool. While that will offer you a very pleasant walk we urge you to resist that temptation.

The exterior may lack kerb appeal, but when you get close enough to glimpse the pool beyond the admission desk even the most hardened of adult swimmers' chins are likely to hit their chests as a soft 'wow' slips out. What lies within is a riot of Mediterranean-resort-style colour and fun. Any children in the party will be completely unable to contain their excitement, so we advise having them changed and ready to go when you arrive so that they can immediately slip your hand and hurl themselves into the water.

The perimeter of the pool is a large lazy river, crisscrossed with gaily painted foot bridges. Inside the lazy river lies an enormous tank, and one smaller pool for young children. The whole thing is a freeform riot of bright white painted concrete, edged in royal blue, that gives the treated river water that fills the pool a hue that is more reminiscent of

Greece than Kent. The water also leaves your skin feeling incredibly soft.

Part of the freeform tank takes on a rectangular shape, so while the dippers and splashers are running riot there is still a functional corner where length swimmers can take their fill.

The jewels in the crown are, however, the slides. We are fans of slides. Even the most curmudgeonly among us can't help but smile upon hitting the water, and a lido slide is essentially a little bit of bottled childhood that we can all recapture. The slides at the Strand are big pink elephants. It takes a special sort of curmudgeon not to grin like a loon while hurtling down a pink elephant's trunk into brilliant clear water.

This is a pool where you can easily make a day of it. There is a lot of space around the pool for setting up base camp with folding chairs and picnic rugs. The changing rooms are utilitarian, and not all the poolside showers work, but none of that matters because the pool itself is a brilliant star. The somewhat counterintuitive opening hours suggest that the local authority managing this pool don't realise quite what an attraction it is. If they grasped the pulling power of a pool like this they would surely open it for longer, and there is a group of volunteer Friends who are working to change that. In the meantime, do check the opening hours on the day you're planning to travel, as they might not be quite what you expect – but this is a pool that is definitely worth the travelling.

This is a great pool for any swimmers with reduced

mobility. The car park is close by, access to the pool buildings is level and firm, as are the pool surrounds, and there are steps with handrails into the tank. The changing rooms are comparatively spacious, which is helpful for wheelchair users.

TONBRIDGE OUTDOOR POOL

ENGLAND Kent

Tonbridge Outdoor Pool
The Slade, Tonbridge
Kent
TN9 1HR

- tonbridge.swimmingpool@tmactive.co.uk
- 01732 367449
- tmactive.co.uk/locations/tonbridge-pool
- @tmactiveleisure
- @TonbridgeSwimmingPool

- 20 m x 13.5 m
- Corporately run on behalf of the council
- Seasonal
- Heated
- Freshwater
- Pay and display car park on site or Lower Castle Fields, Bradford Street, Upper Castle Fields, Lambert's Yard and River Lawn car parks all within walking distance
- On-site café

This modern 1980s leisure centre building in the middle of Tonbridge, by the river, is another of those 'I wasn't expecting this...' outdoor swimming experiences. It's impossible to be unimpressed at how much of an outdoor swimming experience the architects of this centre have managed to create, in a relatively small footprint, by clever use of space with a nod to a traditional model of swimming outside.

Clearly signposted as Tonbridge Swimming Pool from the castle in the centre of town, if you are on foot, and with pay and display parking spaces outside the pool if arriving by car, this unassuming building is on the edge of other outdoor sports facilities. Inside you move seamlessly through reception to a compact changing village where there are separate male and female changing rooms directly opposite standard-sized lockers. Provision for disabled swimmers is very good at this pool, and you should find all needs are met.

And then you are straight out into the outdoor pool environment. The outside 20-metre swimming experience is directly linked to the inside 25-metre pool (next to a separate learner pool) so you can swim between the two by exiting out through an opening in the wall and onwards under a bridge. As a result this is, essentially, one swimming pool split into inside and outside areas, the heated water of both is the same temperature.

The pools are surrounded by areas to sit at tables and relax post-swim, with a mix of grass and paving flanked by the pool buildings on two sides and trees beyond the wall on the others.

WALPOLE BAY TIDAL POOL

ENGLAND Kent

Walpole Bay Tidal Pool
Fifth Avenue, Cliftonville, Margate
Kent
CT9 2JN

- walpole.bay.swimmers@mail.com
- None
- None
- @WalpoleBaySwim
- facebook.com/walpolebayswimmers/
- @walpolebayswimmers

- 16,187 sq m
- Volunteer run
- Year round
- Unheated
- Saltwater
- Limited on-street parking
- None available

At high tide the water completely obliterates Walpole Bay Tidal Pool. As a result, a visit to Margate to swim on spec in this amazing, huge, salty pool can leave you feeling that you've missed something if you come at the wrong time. You'll know it's there, but you won't be able to see it. So, there's a big 'note to self' that comes with deciding to go for a swim at Walpole Bay – check the tide times online and make sure that you are going to be there within a couple of hours either side of low tide.

Confusingly, if you are a first-time visitor to Margate, you might see a tower on the seafront that has the look of a fairground ride crossed with a lighthouse. It has the word 'lido' emblazoned on it, and you might think you've found the tidal pool. Sadly, you'd be mistaken. This marks the site of a now filled-in, abandoned lido,

whose semicircular shape, cast in concrete, still juts out into the sea. The air of decay about the place is a powerful reminder of all the open-air pools that have been lost over the years.

You need to head further south along the esplanade, towards Cliftonville, to find Walpole Bay. There is lots of free parking on the top of the cliff and some lovely artisan shops, cafés and second-hand shops to visit in Cliftonville if you need to pass the time waiting for the tide to ebb away. A brutally ugly set of concrete steps down to the lower esplanade will give you a breathtaking view of the pool and they are the best way to appreciate the scale of the place. The only alternative to the steps is a steeply sloping path that, combined with the sand at beach level, will make this pool challenging to access for disabled swimmers.

A refreshing dip on a warm day, a brisk swim on a bracing day or a triathlon training session in a wetsuit and goggles are all possibilities at this pool, and any children with you will enjoy jumping in from the sea wall opposite the beach where the water is deep and ladders will help them climb out.

There are no changing facilities, and no lifeguard, so your decision to swim here needs to be one where you've taken care of your belongings by leaving most of them behind. It also needs to involve a good wriggle into swimmers under a towel or Dryrobe. And please don't forget that this is a tidal pool; it is easy to get so carried away

with a swim that you forget to keep an eye on the water level in the pool, only to find that the clothes you've left on a clean, dry bit of sand are now submerged by the rising tide! Not that the authors have had this experience... much.

A lido road trip that takes in Walpole Bay Tidal Pool would fit with swims at the stunning and surprising Gillingham Strand Leisure Pool, and Faversham and Tonbridge Outdoor Pools – one road trip and four completely different swims.

HOOD PARK OUTDOOR POOL

ENGLAND Leicestershire

Hood Park Outdoor Pool
North Street, Ashby-de-la-Zouch
Leicestershire
LE65 1HU

- hoodparklc@nwleicestershire.gov.uk
- 01530 412181
- nwleics.gov.uk/pages/hood_park
- @HoodPark_LC
- @hoodparklc

- 33 m x 17 m
- Council run
- Seasonal
- Heated
- Freshwater
- Parking available on site
- On-site café

In all of the Adrian Mole books we read as teenagers, we never once saw a reference to the open-air pool in his home town of Ashby-de-la-Zouch. Could spending his teenage years there have transformed them? Although it might have left us with a much less humourous read!

This is such an easy pool to get to from the A42/M42 in Leicestershire that it would make an ideal stop if you were heading along here between destinations on the M5 and M1 in the Midlands. You wouldn't think there was an open-air swimming pool here as you drive along this motorway/dual carriageway – although, let's face it, that is the basic premise of this book – if we all knew where to find these open-air pool gems there would be no need for this guide!

At 33 metres long, and part of Hood Park Leisure Centre, which offers indoor swimming and other sports and exercise facilities, this is a lovely, heated pool in the centre of town with well-priced pay and display parking close by and shops and cafés around for post-swim cuppas and food. It is another of those locations that you know you've heard of. While you may not have had lots of reasons to visit Ashby previously, you're likely to come away feeling it is a place (and a swim) you'd like to revisit.

This is an efficient place to have a swim – the changing rooms, locker areas and showers are all located poolside where access is level. The outdoor pool is easy to get to out of a side door and there is good, level access, with disabled facilities (including a hoist) and gently sloping steps into the pool. Lounging space is somewhat limited, poolside, but there are some chairs and tables available.

BILLINGHAY SWIMMING POOL

ENGLAND Lincolnshire

Billinghay Swimming Pool
Fen Road, Billinghay
Lincolnshire
LN4 4HU

- None
- 01526 861383
- billinghaypool.blogspot.co.uk
- @BillinghayPool
- Billinghay And District Community Swimming Pool

- 25 m x 10 m
- Volunteer run
- Seasonal
- Heated
- Freshwater
- Parking available on site
- Snack kiosk

You are likely to arrive at Billinghay not really knowing what to expect. It isn't a well-known pool, which is something the other pools in the Lincolnshire cluster, at Skegness, Bourne, Heckington, Metheringham and Woodhall Spa, all seem to have in common. That lack of profile is undeserved, although perhaps understandable given that geographically this part of the UK remains comparatively remote by virtue of having no easy motorway access. That lends an air of travelling back in time a little, with farm stands and village shops seeming to fare better here than elsewhere.

Billinghay is a village that epitomises all of that, with the added bonus of having a glorious community-run outdoor pool at its heart. The buildings attached to the pool are little more than portacabins, but the very best has been made of them, with a cheerfully amusing mural pointing you to 'Skegvegas' on the outside and brightly painted changing rooms and a kiosk/admission desk inside. The kiosk is particularly well stocked, so do make use of it rather than bringing a picnic – small pools like this rely heavily on additional income from food sales.

The pool itself has a slide, which is marked as being open to 'children of all ages'. It's a real pleasure to see adults being encouraged to get in touch with their inner child like this. The pool is open for various sessions throughout the day, so do check the opening times carefully before visiting to make sure you time it right.

We talk a lot about pride and passion among pool volunteers in this book, and both are palpable at Billinghay; it is clearly a much-cherished pool where the lifeguards know the local children's names and invariably go for the gentle word in the ear rather than relying on the whistle to maintain order. The pool is entirely welcoming to non-villagers however, and this is a great destination for a lido road trip, with pleasant gardens in which to while away a little time after your swim.

There is parking right outside the pool and level access. Access to the pool is via ladders. The indoor changing areas are relatively spacious, but not specifically adapted for disabled users.

BOURNE OUTDOOR SWIMMING POOL

ENGLAND Lincolnshire

Bourne Outdoor Swimming Pool
Abbey Lawns, Abbey Road, Bourne
Lincolnshire
PE10 9EP

- enquiries@bourneoutdoorswimmingpool.org
- 01778 422063
- bourneoutdoorswimmingpool.org
- @bournepool
- @bourneoutdoorswimmingpool
- @bourneoutdoorpool

- 48 m x 15 m
- Volunteer run
- Seasonal
- Heated
- Freshwater
- On-street parking
- Snack kiosk

Pools express their characters in a multitude of ways; it's not all about the hole in the ground full of water. The grounds, the people, the views, and any extra facilities like play areas and saunas all play a part, as do smaller, more individual elements like those found at Bourne.

Bourne is a big, period concrete lido with very distinctive geometrically stepped access at the shallow end. That's a design feature, enhanced by the monochromatic paintwork outlining the edge of each step, that we haven't seen anywhere else. It looks fabulous from poolside, but even more striking

if you can look at it underwater and, of course, the steps provide good access for people not comfortable using ladders. Gorgeous manicured gardens surround the pool. It has good indoor changing rooms, tucked away in a corner of the site, and a shady seating area running alongside the length of the pool.

These things are all part of Bourne's unique identity, certainly, but Bourne's particular quirk is its signage. It's hard to be individual in this area, as pools often boast a forest of health and safety-related signage. No running, no diving, no photography, and so on. And on. Bourne has all of those familiar notices, and a lot of them. Look around and you'll see a sign of some sort every few feet. But it isn't the volume that is unique. There are also quirky one-offs that you wouldn't see anywhere else. Our favourite is the plaque on the wall of the plant room that really brings home the community love of, and involvement with, this gem of a pool; it commemorates the funds being raised for the first heating system in 1971.

We're not highlighting the signage as a negative, but as a perfect example of something that is a hallmark of outdoor pools when they are set against indoor pools – namely personality. Personality expressed in small details. Bourne illustrates the rewards that can be had when you take time to see details. It's easy to dismiss signage as visual clutter, and to pay it no attention. But at outdoor pools looking at, and seeing, the small things very often reveals something individual and wonderful about a pool's character.

EMBASSY POOL/SKEGNESS OUTDOOR POOL

ENGLAND Lincolnshire

Embassy Pool/Skegness Outdoor Pool
Grand Parade, Skegness
Lincolnshire
PE25 2UG

- skegnesspool@mvtlc.org
- 01754 610675
- magnavitae.org/venue/skegness-pool-fitness-suite
- @Skegness_SP
- @SkegnessSwimmingPool

- 25 m x 13 m
- Corporately run on behalf of the council
- Seasonal
- Heated
- Freshwater
- Pay and display car park on site
- Snack kiosk

You will all have preconceived ideas about Skegness; notions of what it once was and what it now is. And many of them will be right. But we can almost guarantee that any preconceived ideas you may have about the outdoor pool will be wrong – particularly if you are imagining the faded glory that is often characteristic of Victorian seaside resorts.

There is much faded glory about the town, but the pool plays no part in that. It lies sandwiched in between the esplanade shops and the funfair, a glistening blue beacon of sophistication sunk into a natural dip that helps to fend off any stiff sea breeze that might be blowing. The setting creates a sheltered suntrap. The entrance is workaday leisure centre in style, and the indoor changing rooms offer good provision for disabled swimmers.

The pool itself is in a different league when set against these humdrum utilitarian buildings. It sits in pleasant grassy grounds, with an abundance of sunloungers contributing to a holiday atmosphere that is entirely in keeping with the location. The pool is ideal for lengths, although it doesn't always have a lane in. Perpendicular to the main tank is a sloping beach-style entry point that is perfect for younger swimmers and those who like the security of a gentle entry. The whole thing is smart and gleamingly modern.

Embassy is the sort of pool that makes you want to linger. You might go planning to just have your swim and leave. On all but the very worst weather days, however, leave yourself some leeway, because you might well be unable to resist the lure of the sunlounger and a snack from the kiosk.

HECKINGTON COMMUNITY SWIMMING POOL

ENGLAND Lincolnshire

Heckington Community Swimming Pool
Howell Road, Heckington
Lincolnshire
NG34 9RX

- info@heckingtonpool.co.uk
- 07895 965883
- heckingtonpool.co.uk
- Heckington Community Swimming Pool

- 15 m x 5 m
- Volunteer run
- Seasonal
- Heated
- Freshwater
- Parking available in the village
- Snack kiosk

Heckington is one of the smallest pools featured in this book, and if you are the sort of swimmer who likes to bash out the lengths and rack up some distance this isn't a pool that is going to make it onto your wish list. But swimmers are a diverse and fascinating group of people, and for every swimmer who isn't drawn to a small village pool there will be others for whom the petite size and uniform depth of Heckington will be a positive selling point.

Heckington is a community pool in every sense of the phrase. It is run by the village that envelops it, and used primarily by that same community. Surrounding the pool are picnic tables, cheerful bunting, a small

marquee for shade and some indoor changing areas that are equally petite. While children play gleefully in the water, adults sit and chat, read newspapers, and perhaps dip in and out of the water to join in the fun. It's a peaceful, uplifting sort of place that the children who live nearby will have powerful and lasting memories of.

But it isn't just a local pool for local people. It's open to the public, albeit with session times that need careful checking on the website before you travel. But the lido chat is plentiful, and you'll be made to feel part of the community for the few hours that you are there. On one of our swims at Heckington there was a woman who had come up from Peterborough with her grandchildren. It's a day trip that they regularly undertake when the children stay over because they like the small pool and community feel of Heckington more than they like the scale and grandeur of the lido in their own town. She was also keen to say that they all felt as though swimming outdoors feels like a treat worth travelling for. One imagines the reasonably priced post-swim ice lollies are just as much a part of the treat for all of them.

Maybe that's the most glorious thing about lidos – they are as fascinating and diverse as the swimmers who use them. So while the small but perfectly formed Heckington pool won't be everybody's cup of tea, it will be a place that some can, and will, fall in love with.

In terms of accessibility there is level access from the street and around the pool. Entry into the tank is via gently sloping steps with a good handrail, and the pool is uniformly 1 metre deep.

JUBILEE PARK WOODHALL SPA

ENGLAND Lincolnshire

Jubilee Park Woodhall Spa
Stixwould Road, Woodhall Spa
Lincolnshire
LN10 6QH

- manager@jubileeparkwoodhallspa.co.uk
- 01526 353478
- jubileeparkwoodhallspa.co.uk
- @JubileeParkWood
- Jubilee Park Woodhall Spa
- @jubilee_park_woodhall_spa

- 33 m x 12 m
- Charitable trust run
- Seasonal
- Heated
- Freshwater
- Parking available on site
- Snack kiosk

Woodhall Spa is a pleasantly genteel small town in the depths of Lincolnshire, and in Jubilee Park it has a spectacular set of facilities that would be the envy of towns several times as large.

The pool is just one part of Jubilee Park, which features beautiful ornamental gardens, sports grounds and a campsite. All this undoubtedly helps the pool to thrive by delivering footfall. It also helps give the pool a distinct holiday feel that makes it the sort of place you are going to want to spend more than just an hour or two.

The changing rooms have some pleasingly vintage 1960s cubicles, with decent accessibility for disabled swimmers, and the original basket store has been retained. You'll be given one of the plastic baskets, cleverly designed to hang a jacket on and keep your trousers crease-free, which you then hand in at the store where it will join the serried ranks of its jaunty fellows. You can, of course, look after your own things if you prefer.

The pool sits in extensive and perfectly manicured gardens that are ideal for spreading out and relaxing. The climbing plant

covered arbour is a particular delight when everything is in bloom. There is a well-stocked kiosk, and some garden furniture at which to enjoy tea.

As lovely as the grounds are, however, they don't overshadow the pool. The main tank is an excellent size, and immaculately kept, with a small slide for children. On all but the very busy days the pool is big enough that you can carve out some space for a decent swim, and there is often a lane in. There are steps with a handrail into the pool, and a hoist is available. There is a second smaller and shallower tank with a brightly coloured water feature in the shape of a giant tap that will rain water onto the heads of delighted young, and young at heart, swimmers.

Jubilee Park feels like a little slice of rose garden English nostalgia, in a very good way indeed.

METHERINGHAM SWIMMING POOL

ENGLAND Lincolnshire

Metheringham Swimming Pool
Prince's Street, Metheringham
Lincolnshire
LN4 3BX

- metheringhamswimmingpool@outlook.com
- 01526 888146
- megpool.org.uk
- @MegPool
- @megpooluk

- 15 m x 8 m
- Volunteer run
- Seasonal
- Heated
- Freshwater
- Neighbouring parish council car park
- Snack kiosk

Lincolnshire is blessed with six outdoor pools, and that makes it the ideal county for a one- or two-day lido road trip. Metheringham is a small village that hosts an outdoor pool next to the primary school, in a park area with swings and slides.

The pool, affectionately known as Meg Pool, offers a decent space to swim laps if it is not too busy, and the poolside slide makes a fun way to enter the water. There is also a pool chair to assist disabled swimmers with entry. The changing rooms offer male and female communal spaces and have a shower, though due to the age and compact nature of the buildings it hasn't been possible for Metheringham to provide a changing area with easy access for wheelchair-using swimmers. There is plenty of space around the pool, complete with tables and chairs, to enjoy a chance to dry off and sit in the sun on a warm day.

This is another pool that is run by happy, chatty and supportive volunteers who keep it going for those who live locally and those who cruise by for a holiday swim. There may be cakes for sale on the day you visit, to help raise funds, and even if there aren't there is a well-stocked snack kiosk offering sweets and drinks at reasonable prices.

There is plenty of free car parking in the village near the pool and a range of different sessions which should leave swimmers of all varieties feeling well catered for.

WARNING!
DEEP
END

BROCKWELL LIDO

ENGLAND London

HISTORIC POOLS OF BRITAIN

Brockwell Lido
Brockwell Park, Dulwich Road
London
SE24 0PA

- bwl-sales@fusion-lifestyle.com
- 02072 743088
- fusion-lifestyle.com/centres/brockwell-lido
- @Brockwell_Lido
- @BrockwellLidoUK
- @brockwell_lido

- 50 m x 25 m
- Corporately run on behalf of the council
- Year round
- Unheated
- Freshwater
- Car park and on-street parking
- On-site café

Brockwell is just one of the London large-scale pools, all of them harking back to days when lidos were seen as a measure of society's success and civilisation, and when spending to build public amenities was a strategy for economic growth. Times have changed a great deal since those heady days, but the remaining London leviathans stand testament to them.

Brockwell is a 50-metre tank, half as wide as it is long. The water is unheated, and while the question of heating is often a divisive one, not least among Brockwell regulars, this is a pool that has embraced the cold. It remains open to the public all year round, with a decent programme of publicly accessible hours. You'll get a very different experience swimming in winter and summer, so this is a pool that is worth revisiting with the seasons.

In summer it is fondly known as Brixton Beach, and one can see why. The extensive terraces become a patchwork of towels, and sun worshippers in their finery are much in evidence. It is clearly a place to see and be seen, and extensive queues are commonplace on hot days. There is a kiosk serving food to swimmers poolside, and the café has an excellent reputation that spreads well beyond the swimming community. Breakfast on the sunny deck, at any time of year, is a considerable treat.

In winter the crowds evaporate, apart from in the café, which is so popular year round with swimmers and non-swimmers alike that booking is advisable if you have little flexibility on time. The cold-water swimming advice is more prominently displayed, and the poolside sauna replaces the terraces as the place to be. That makes for an altogether more personal experience, as it's hard to sit shivering in a sauna without striking up some conversation. If you get chatting to a regular swimmer you'll very quickly come to learn just how passionate they are about this pool – and quite rightly so: it's marvellous.

The pool has good provision for disabled swimmers in the changing areas, and the poolside area (with the exception of a small area of raised decking) is level all round. There are gently sloping steps, with a handrail, into the shallow end. There is a disability hoist available, and any swimmers wishing to use it should speak to the duty manager to coordinate that.

CHARLTON LIDO

ENGLAND London

Charlton Lido
Hornfair Park, Shooters Hill Road, Greenwich
London
SE18 4LX

- charltonlido@gll.org
- 0208 856 7389
- better.org.uk/leisure-centre/london/greenwich/charlton-lido
- Pool: @charltonlido
  Friends association: @FoCLSE7
- @charltonlido
- @charltonlidolifestyle

- 50 m x 20 m
- Corporately run on behalf of the council
- Year round
- Heated
- Freshwater
- Car park and on-street parking
- On-site café

South London isn't blessed with as many lidos as north London, but the pools it does have are impressive in terms of both scale and atmosphere.

Charlton is cut from the same cloth as Parliament Hill and Brockwell, and while it is less similar to those two pools than they are to each other, you'll notice some architectural resonance in places. What really makes Charlton stand out, however, is heating. This is a big pool, by anybody's standards, and to have it heated year round, and open with extensive hours even in winter, is a rare treat and that alone would make it worthy of a visit. Throw in the abundant, free, unrestricted on-street parking close to the pool and it is an ideal destination for a winter lido road trip.

In summer Charlton becomes a slightly different beast. On hot

days the paved areas become so thick with spread-out towels that it can be slightly challenging to navigate your way across poolside without stepping on someone else's territory. But the size of the pool, and the way the space is managed, means that you are still highly likely to get a decent swim in. There are always lanes in, labelled fast, medium, slow, and the rest of the tank is subdivided to allow for less confident swimmers to have a safe space in the shallow end while more boisterous swimmers can fling themselves into the deep end with joyous abandon.

The changing rooms sit alongside the pool, and one has to leave the entrance block and walk around the pool to reach them. The café is also accessed from poolside, via some stairs to the roof terrace on top of the block. The café is a fairly typical offering from corporate operators, functional but uninspiring. The roof terrace, however, is a thing of joy. On the far side of the café members have their own roof terrace with swish furniture. The plastic furniture on the public side of the terrace is more utilitarian, but the location is no less lovely. The roof terrace is a real suntrap, and the views down to the pool are beautiful and really give a sense of the size of the site. It also offers the best view of the traditional fountains at the far end of the site. Whatever the weather when you visit, you won't regret expending the effort to climb the stairs and drink it in. Charlton is a very accessible pool, with dedicated changing and toilets, level access around the site, a disability hoist and a lift to the café and sun terraces.

FINCHLEY LIDO

ENGLAND London

Finchley Lido

Great North Leisure Park, Chaplin Square, Finchley

London

N12 0GL

finchley-lido@gll.org

020 8343 9830

better.org.uk/leisure-centre/london/barnet/finchley-lido-leisure-centre

Finchley Lido Leisure Centre

25 m x 10 m

Corporately run on behalf of the council

Seasonal

Unheated

Freshwater

Parking available on site

Snack shop

Finchley can only be seen as the palest shadow of a nod to the mighty Larkswood, a stunning cruciform lido of high Art Deco style that once stood in this area. It has been replaced, sadly but not uncommonly, with a spiritually and aesthetically empty modern leisure centre surrounded by chain restaurants. Pulling into the car park will leave you doubting that you can possibly be in the right place to find a lido.

And it is debatable whether Finchley can truly be called a lido; it falls on the cusp and we believe in giving the benefit of the doubt, so it makes this guide by the skin of its teeth. It has grassy surrounds for sunbathing, which helps its cause, it has gentle stepped access, and it is long enough to swim some lengths. This all tips the scales in its favour.

Finchley is, however, only two lanes wide, with the perpendicular stepped area at one end. It looks like the sort of lap pool one might find in the garden of a smart holiday villa. Its opening hours are meek, and often don't conform to what is shown on the website. If you live locally it's a better-than-nothing lido where families might enjoy bringing children for a dip and a splash, but as a lido road trip destination it is only likely to be of interest to the most hardened of lido collectors. If you are travelling, ring ahead and even then be prepared for disappointment, as it appears to be closed if the smallest of clouds or most passing of showers streak the sky. Between us we visited several times before we actually found the outdoor pool open, despite having called ahead, and the indoor pool could in no way be considered a consolation.

It is well set up for disabled swimmers, although there is no hoist to access the outdoor pool.

HAMPSTEAD HEATH BATHING PONDS

ENGLAND London

Hampstead Heath Bathing Ponds
Hampstead Heath
London

Hampstead.heath@cityoflondon.gov.uk
020 7485 5757
cityoflondon.gov.uk/things-to-do/green-spaces/hampstead-heath/swimming
@cityoflondon
Hampstead Ponds
@colhampsteadheath

Irregular
Council run
Year round
Unheated
Freshwater
Car park and on-street parking available but not immediately on site (good public transport links, some walking also required)
None

Mixed Bathing Pond, Highgate Men's Pond, Kenwood Ladies' Swimming Pond

Throughout the thinking about, planning and writing of *The Lido Guide* there has been significant debate about whether or not the three public-access swimming ponds on Hampstead Heath in London qualify as lidos, or whether they verge more on wild swims. We've always come down on the side of swims that are, perhaps, too wild to meet the criteria for this book. These three swimming pools are naturally occurring open water spaces and we've specifically defined a lido as having a man-made element to it. Until summer 2018.

So, what persuaded us to include them? Primarily, we swam in them! We'd already noted that Oliver Merrington, Janet Smith and Kate Rew had ALL classified the Hampstead Heath Ponds as lidos, and we've already mentioned what inspiration their work on identifying lidos has been for us. And Janet's 1990s devotion to Parliament Hill Lido, also situated on Hampstead Heath, gave rise to her quest to know about more open-air pools in the capital and across the UK. In 2018 the copious sunshine brought the ponds into sharper focus, with social media highlighting them as popular public-access swimming pools with lifeguards and changing facilities. That made us think again, so off Janet went armed with her cossie and a towel to check them out.

We're embarrassed, now, to admit that we'd originally dismissed them as not being lidos without ever going to check. Not least as swimming, and checking (then swimming and checking again) have been cornerstones of the research for this guide.

And so this book comes full circle to Hampstead Heath in London.

There are three ponds, all of which give the opportunity of long, languorous swims in the open air in the middle of the city. You may be forgiven for assuming that you'll find them all co-located on Hampstead Heath. In fact, they are nothing of the sort and you'll also find that you can't swim all three although there's a lovely walking trip to be had swimming in two AND Parliament Hill Lido without leaving the confines of the Heath.

So, why can't you swim in all three? Well, one is for all swimmers – the mixed pond – and the others are gender-segregated ponds – the men's pond and the Kenwood Ladies'

swimming pond. We hear that there are occasional opportunities for women to swim at the men's pond, they are worth looking out for as they aren't frequent.

The mixed pond, within a 10–15 minute walking distance of Hampstead Heath Overground station, is for all. This large swimming pond can be clearly viewed from the man-made causeway that boundaries the south end of the pond. A short walk up the eastern side of it brings you to the entrance, payment machine, lifeguards' hut and changing rooms/toilets. In some respects, it is feels surprising to pay for a swim in a pond, but it becomes immediately obvious that you aren't paying for the full value of your swim but making a small contribution to a well-maintained swimming facility that has lifeguards on duty during all opening hours.

Entry to the pond is via a choice of long metal ladders that stretch into the deep, cool, green water from the jetty; there's no diving allowed here. Clearly cordoned swimming areas with lifebuoys help you to see where you can swim languidly,

vigorously or putter as you please. The lifeguards will check your knowledge and experience of this type of swimming (and that of any accompanying children) before you get in and will be pleasant and courteous about your swimming ability and related safety. Post-swim, there are open-air showers on the bank where your thoughts may stray to the idea of swimming here year-round with a season ticket. Mainly though, day tickets provide casual opportunities to swim here.

If anything, the men's pond offers even more lido-like opportunities than the mixed pond. With the similar changing block and lifeguard set up, this pond is huge AND has a springboard for diving and/or jumping into the water as well as the pond-side ladders. Located on the east side of the Heath and closer to Highgate than Hampstead, there are plenty of opportunities to admire this swimming spot from the pathways that circle it even if you are not eligible to swim in it!

All the ponds charge the same, nominal amount for entry, but for this you can stay all day. They are all run in a similar way despite being very different entities. The Kenwood Ladies' Pond has the most modern changing facilities and as far as we could tell was the only one with a pond-side winch for disabled access, although the lack of close vehicle access might be difficult for some to negotiate. The ladies' pond is the most sheltered, secluded and smallest of the three and yet still big enough for a long swim.

If you have swum in a few open-air pools by now you'll already have noticed how similar entities, with the same purpose, can be so varied and a trip to one or two of the Hampstead Heath Ponds will reinforce that *same-but-different* feeling. Outdoor pools all have open-air water, for the purpose of leisure and swimming, but how many different manifestations can it have? Well, at least 130 in the UK and Channel Islands for a start! Walking away, after refreshing *can't-see-or-touch-the-bottom-or-the-sides-but-it-didn't-matter swims*, it was plain that the ponds definitely fit the criteria of being lidos; Oliver, Janet, Kate – you were right.

HAMPTON POOL

ENGLAND London

Hampton Pool
High Street, Hampton
London
TW12 2ST

- info@hamptonpool.co.uk
- 020 8255 1116
- hamptonpool.co.uk
- @HamptonPool
- @hamptonpooltw12
- @hamptonpool

- 36.5 m x 14 m
- Charitable trust run
- Year round
- Heated
- Freshwater
- Small car park and on-street parking
- On-site café

Hampton Pool is one of those full-ticket lido experiences where you can swim outside in a freshwater heated pool every single day of the year. What lido lover could ask for anything more?

Run as a commercial enterprise by the YMCA, in conjunction with the voluntary Hampton Pool Trust, this is a pool that has other leisure and sports facilities on site but whose main attraction for visitors and locals alike must be the large 36.5-by-14-metre pool at its centre, with an additional smaller pool (12 by 7 metres) for children.

Set in a large grassy area, this pool opens through sunshine and snow, rain and wind, early morning for pre-work swims and late into the night for movie nights and special occasions. It runs lane sessions, inflatable fun sessions and classes, and is the kind of pool where almost every type of swimmer or lido enthusiast can find something to really enjoy during a visit.

Changing rooms shared with the gym/leisure side of the facilities provide cubicles and lockers inside the entry buildings, and there is also a poolside café serving a variety of food, drinks and snacks for visitors.

The pool is within walking distance of Hampton station, which might be the better way to get there, as although free parking is available on site, it is limited. It makes a good combination of a lido road trip with Richmond's Pools in the Park or Guildford Lido if you are heading along the south-west portion of the M25.

Hampton has sloping step access with handrails into both pools and a hoist is also available that can be used for both pools. There is a disabled-accessible changing room, with its own toilet, and good level access around the site.

HILLINGDON LIDO

ENGLAND London

HISTORIC POOLS OF BRITAIN

Hillingdon Lido
Gatting Way, Park Road, Uxbridge
London
UB8 1ES

hslc-sales@fusion-lifestyle.com
03451 307324
fusion-lifestyle.com/centres/hillingdon-sport-and-leisure-complex/your-centre/lido/
@HillingdonSLC
@HillingdonSLC

50 m x 20 m
Corporately run on behalf of the council
Year round
Unheated
Freshwater
Parking available on site
On-site café

There is something rather breathtaking about Hillingdon Lido (formerly known as Uxbridge Lido). Restored and run by leisure company Fusion, which has played a significant part in bringing this and other lidos back to life, this is a pool that has everything that you'd want from a 50-metre lido. There is something quite spectacular about it.

Entry from the pay and display car park outside or by bus from Uxbridge station takes you up a sweeping walkway towards the large and welcoming entrance of the Art Deco-style building and foyer, where you can see the pool on your right-hand side through big windows as you queue to get in. At this point it is worth saying that it is useful to be clear about what you want when you get to the front of the queue, as there are various add-ons to the entrance price to swim and dithering at the front of the queue tends to garner tuts from regular users! What do we mean by add-ons? Mainly whether you want to have fun with the inflatables or hire a sunlounger.

Changing for the outdoor pool runs the length of the pool and there are banks of very conveniently placed, decent-sized lockers opposite the changing cubicles. Toilets are also located poolside, so on very busy days where there is a separate entrance for lido users only, you have a self-contained experience in the outside lido world. As you would expect from a relatively modern restoration, there is very good disabled-access provision across the board.

Entry to the pool can only be described as refreshing. At 20 metres wide and 50 metres long, there is a lot of water in this pool, whose deep section is in the middle, and none of it is heated. There are smaller pools at the top of the main tank for little ones, and the water here is warmer.

The glory of a long swim in this pool garners superlatives. It is a memorable swimming experience. The water is sparkling and clean and the bottom of the tank is a glorious blue. The buildings around you are a bright white and, on a sunny day, this all adds up to a classic lido experience. One of the things about a large, commercial leisure environment is that many things are often going on simultaneously. Here it felt completely natural to have children playing on the inflatable courses and music pumping out for what looked like a pretty tough exercise class while swimming up and down the pool thinking, noticing and simultaneously being undisturbed by it all.

Hillingdon Lido was closed for a number of years, and the scale of the restoration is clear once you compare your experience and views with photos of what the pool looked like in a derelict state. It's appropriate, here, for us to nod in recognition of the work it takes to create a facility like this. It's a privilege to be able to swim in this restored beauty; we're only able to do so because, as with the majority of open-air pools across the country, someone believes enough to generate the enthusiasm of others, create a vision of what is possible, and put the hours in, so many of them unpaid. Those early, passionate people paved the way for us all. Thanks to them, we can enjoy an outdoor swimming experience that will linger long in the memory.

LONDON FIELDS LIDO

ENGLAND London

London Fields Lido
London Fields West Side, Hackney
London
E8 3EU

- london-fields-lido@gll.org
- 02072 549038
- better.org.uk/leisure-centre/london/hackney/london-fields-lido
- @LondonFieldLido
- London Fields Lido

- 50 m x 20 m
- Corporately run on behalf of the council
- Year round
- Heated
- Freshwater
- On-street parking
- On-site café

One of the many blessings of living in London is the vast choice of open-air pools available. Compared to, for example, the whole of Wales, where only one lido is currently open, Londoners are beyond well served. And they are served by pools that also offer a variety of purpose. If you are a serious swimmer who prefers a pool to be racked out with largely well-managed lanes, then London Fields is the pool for you – not least as floodlighting and heating means it can offer perhaps the most extensive opening hours of all the London pools right through the year.

Its history is little short of miraculous. Near derelict for years, it was fully restored before reopening in 2006, and then further extensively refurbished in 2017. The result is a gleaming, modern, purposeful mecca for the committed swimmer. You don't, of course, need to be a hardcore training junkie to swim here; there is a wide lane for the more social swimmer. You'll enjoy the quiet, steady, rhythmic soundscape of other swimmers ploughing up and down, the high standard of the facility, the easy-access sloped walk into the pool and the neat, bright clean surroundings that still retain a hint of period charm. You can expect, however, to be cheek by jowl with pull buoys, kickboards and isotonic-drink-filled water bottles at pretty much all times.

This isn't a pool that should be top of your list for a family day out, unless you are a swimming family who travel with your own individual laminated set cards, but if you can move yourself to swim in a serenely purposeful manner then this pool is definitely worth a visit. Disabled swimmers will find that London Fields caters well for them, with accessible changing areas, level access throughout and a hoist to supplement the sloped access into the tank.

OASIS OUTDOOR POOL

ENGLAND London

Oasis Outdoor Pool
32 Endell Street, Covent Garden
London
WC2H 9AG

- oasis@gll.org
- 020 7831 1804
- better.org.uk/leisure-centre/london/camden/oasis-sports-centre
- @OasisSportsCentre

- 27.5 m x 10 m
- Corporately run on behalf of the council
- Year round
- Heated
- Freshwater
- On-street parking
- On-site café

The location of Oasis, tucked away in the heart of theatreland, is perhaps the most unexpected thing about it, but the surprises don't end at the door. It is, in truth, easy to miss the door, given that it is a bland and characterless commercial-looking entrance up a few steps off a busy street. There is a sign, clearly visible above the door, but you'll need to look up to be sure you spot it. Even on a second or third visit it is easy to walk straight past, and in some ways the anonymous nature of the entrance lends a little to Oasis' ample charms.

At the reception desk very little is given away about what awaits you. If the café area isn't busy you might just catch a tantalising glimpse of a flash of blue. You then divert away, and down some stairs, to a very smart changing area. You will need change for the lockers, and you need to be aware that you won't get your locker money back when you reopen it, so ducking back to your locker for something mid-visit will require having some extra coins handy. That feels a bit churlish, but the admission is excellent value and it's unlikely you'll go away feeling hard done by for the loss of your small change.

As you ascend the stairs to the pool there is no shying away from the fact that you are leaving the swishness of the changing area behind you. The stairwell, and the tank, could use a little refurbishment, but were it not for the standard of the changing rooms you probably wouldn't even notice that. You'll see the indoor pool first, but press on through the door and the outdoor pool will fall at your feet. It is, effectively, a rooftop pool, albeit one surrounded by taller buildings.

It is often busiest in the early mornings and early evenings, as it is popular with swimmers who work nearby, but there is a lane system in place that includes a social/casual lane, and some of the lifeguards are very good at managing the lanes to maintain some harmony. If you go at a busy time, however, do expect to be rubbing shoulders, possibly literally, with a number of fellow swimmers.

In winter the pool is a particular joy, as the dragon's breath rises from the heated water and the poolside sauna comes into its own. Whatever time of year you visit, do take some time to float on your back and look up at the parcel of sky, stark against the buildings that wrap it. Whether it is bright blue, riveted with scudding clouds or pinpricked with stars, it is a sight that brings home what a unique and special pool this is to have right in the heart of the capital.

Swimmers with reduced mobility shouldn't feel put off by all the talk of steps and stairs in this entry. There is good provision, with wheelchair access, dedicated facilities that negate the stairs, and a hoist is available to access the pool.

PARK ROAD POOLS AND FITNESS

ENGLAND London

Park Road Pools and Fitness
Park Road
London
N8 8JN

prlc-sales@fusion-lifestyle.com
020 8341 3567
fusion-lifestyle.com/centres/park-road-pools-fitness
@PR_PoolsFitness
@ParkroadPF
@parkroadpoolsandfitness

- 50 m x 23 m
- Corporately run on behalf of the council
- Year round
- Heated
- Freshwater
- Parking available on site
- On-site café

This is among the biggest heated outdoor pools in the UK (along with Charlton Lido in south-east London and Woodgreen Lido in Banbury). At 50 metres by 23 metres it is a large expanse of water surrounded by grassy banks on which to while away the day either side of a serious lap swim or some fun play in the water. It has been here since 1926, although the toddler pool seems to be a more recent addition.

As it's been closed for renovation for a couple of years it is wonderful to see this pool restored to a great outdoor space for locals and visitors to north London, and in early 2018 the pool tank benefited from further refurbishment. The lido is a fantastic addition to the modern leisure centre it is attached to, which also houses an indoor 25-metre pool and learner pool, as well as a gym and other facilities. It is run by Fusion, which understands open-air pools in the UK, and has great knowledge and experience of running other lidos across the country. Entry to the lido isn't through the main entrance, but through a turnstile in the fence to one side of the building.

There is the standard changing village approach at Park Road, with lockers and on-site refreshments to accompany your swim. Being run as

part of a larger leisure centre facilitates some decent opening times for the pool and there are sessions for lane swimming, exercise classes and fun for all the family. Disabled access is good, with dedicated changing facilities. There is no hoist into the outdoor pool, however.

This is a great lido. It never really seems to make it on to any top ten lists, and yet it's a swimming gem tucked inside the North Circular road in London, not far from the A1. It would make a very decent lido road trip in conjunction with nearby London Fields Lido in Hackney and Parliament Hill Lido on Hampstead Heath.

PARLIAMENT HILL LIDO

ENGLAND London

Parliament Hill Lido
Heath Lodge, Hampstead
London
NW5 1NA

hampstead.heath@cityoflondon.gov.uk
020 7485 3873
cityoflondon.gov.uk/things-to-do/green-spaces/hampstead-heath/swimming/
@LidoPh
Parliament Hill Lido

61 m x 27 m
Council run
Year round
Unheated
Freshwater
Pay and display car park on site
On-site café

© Roger Taylor

Hampstead Heath holds a special place in the heart of many Londoners, with its wide-open spaces and unrivalled elevated view of the capital. It also holds a special place in the heart of many swimmers, being home to Hampstead Heath Bathing Ponds and Parliament Hill Lido. The former offer a wild(ish) swim experience within easy reach of the city centre while the lido, a relatively short walk from the bathing ponds, offers a swim that is absolutely unique.

The lido buildings themselves are, essentially, a scaled-up version of Brockwell. If you've swum at both pools the identical brickwork and styling of the architecture cannot have escaped you. The digital water/air temperature display that greets you after you pass through the turnstile is an iconic feature of Parliament Hill Lido, and it will be a familiar sight to even the most casual follower of social media swimming groups, where selfies with the display are a regular feature. If you're familiar with that imagery, but haven't actually swum at the pool, it will feel a little like being greeted by an old friend.

The changing rooms at Parliament Hill are rather down at heel, lagging behind their refurbished cousins at most

other London pools. The cubicle doors are no longer there, and there is an air of shabby chic that pushes the concept to the very limit. There is, however, plenty of space for wheelchair users (who are also well served by the ramped access to the entrance), a fine set of communal hot showers and a heat lamp that knocks the edge off the chill in winter – as does the poolside sauna. This is one of a very small number of pools to have retained a staffed basket store, so you can safely leave valuables under the stewardship of the attendant before you make your way onto poolside.

The pool area is vast and largely level, and in summer the atmosphere is heady as what sometimes feels like all of London descends on Parliament Hill. Crowd control is as much a part of a lifeguard's job here as is water safety, and they do an excellent job of it. There is a small baby pool, the obligatory wedding-cake fountain that many London pools have thoughtfully preserved and a café that, while subject to what feels like frequent changes of tenant, always has an interesting selection of often home-made food available.

What really makes this pool unique, however, won't be readily apparent until you are looking straight down into the vast tank or until you dive right in. (If diving isn't for you, there are gently sloping steps with a handrail, a hoist and ladders to make use of instead.) The pool has been relined with what is, essentially, a stainless-steel box that creates a shimmering deck-level swim with an underwater view that will not be found in any other UK lido. In summer it glitters and sparkles like the scales on a mermaid's tale. There are no lane lines, so swimming lengths requires the ability to follow a line of the dimples that texture the bottom – and an ability to break out of the hypnotic reverie that the light dappling the steel creates in order to cast your eye about for other swimmers approaching. Looking forward, the colour of the blue is reminiscent of swimming in the deep ocean. In winter, that blue seems to deepen and darken as the water temperature falls. In the depths of January, it feels like swimming inside a Fox's Glacier Mint.

Whatever time of year you swim here, that colour, the sensory treat of that unique blue, will surpass any issue you might have with the shabby changing rooms. You will fall instantly, overwhelmingly and completely in love.

POOLS ON THE PARK

ENGLAND London

Pools on the Park
Old Deer Park, Twickenham Road, Richmond
London
TW9 2SF

- leisure@richmond.gov.uk
- 020 3772 2999
- richmond.gov.uk/pools_on_the_park
- @poolsonthepark
- @FGFPoolsonthePark
- @poolsonthepark

- 33 m x 13 m
- Corporately run on behalf of the council
- Year round
- Heated
- Freshwater
- Neighbouring public car park
- On-site café

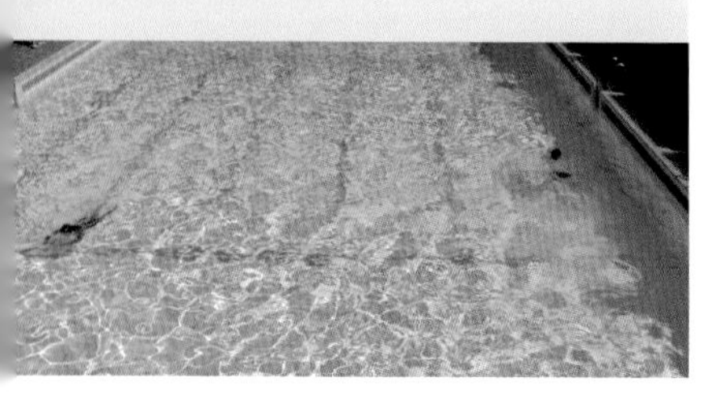

© Jo Pond

Some of the lidos in this book are relatively difficult to find on the first visit, and in many ways the feeling that you've discovered something is what makes them special. By contrast, Richmond's Pools on the Park is one of the most straightforward to get to. It's situated on the A316 main road from Twickenham into central London, within walking distance of Richmond station on both tube and main lines or on a bus route that stops outside the entrance. This isn't to say that it's easy to swim in this pool if you live in Inverness, Aberystwyth or Grimbsy – just that it is among the easier of the pools to locate, with multiple transport options.

We've written elsewhere in the guide that the majority of lidos are in the south of England, and London definitely punches above its weight in terms of heated and unheated, modern and

© Jo Pond

traditional open-air pools. If you happen to be, or live, in London, the opportunity to swim at Pools on the Park is a treat, and as of winter 2017/2018 that treat is now available year round.

The large, sparkling pool with grassy and paved poolside areas, a terrace overlooking the lido and the opportunity of a decent swim in this 33-metre tank all add up to a good experience. This is part of a large leisure centre where there are also indoor 25-metre and learner pools and the changing village so familiar to leisure-centre users. As you'd expect of a facility like this, disability access provision is good, with dedicated changing areas, level access to the pools and tiled steps that run the entire width of the shallow end. There are handrails, plus a hoist that can be used in all the pools. There are warm showers and lockers that require the purchase of a token at reception to use (this is both non-refundable AND like no other token you've seen for any other locker elsewhere!). There is space around the pool for you to take your belongings with you, and if you've parked your car in the pay and display car park outside the door, valuables are probably best left in your locked car if you don't want the faff of the locker token.

Although there is a café and refreshments on site you are within walking distance of Richmond's high street and its cafés, shops and restaurants, or bring a picnic with you – just be aware that this, like a number of the London lidos, is one of those pools where you might be subject to a queue and bag search on entry at busy times.

© Jo Pond

SERPENTINE LIDO

ENGLAND London

Serpentine Lido
Hyde Park, South Carriage Drive
London
W2 2UH

- None
- 020 7706 3422
- royalparks.org.uk/parks/hyde-park/things-to-see-and-do/sports-and-leisure/serpentine-lido
- @theroyalparks
- @serpentinelido
- @theroyalparks

- 100 m x 30 m
- Royal Parks
- Seasonal
- Unheated
- Freshwater
- Pay and display parking available on West Carriage Drive and in car parks at either end of Serpentine Bridge
- On-site café

Is the Serpentine really a lido? Oh, yes... and not just because it tells you that it is! Situated in the centre of Hyde Park, this is a designated swimming spot that always seems to feature on the news on the hottest or coldest days of the year, when there will be members of the Serpentine Swimming Club, who swim year round regardless of the weather, taking a dip in front of the cameras.

So, this is a lido that we've known about for years; *Blue Peter* presenters of several generations have swum here, generally when it's chilly, but in the summer this is a great spot for a proper swim within the cordoned-off area of the Serpentine.

Entry is through the reception building of the lido, through to lockers and changing rooms; lifeguards can open a gate to the beach area, so steps can be avoided if needed. The changing rooms are a bit on the small side, but do the job, and there is a warm shower for when you get

out. There is a disabled toilet that has a bench and is big enough to be used for changing.

The water is clean and clear on the surface, but in the deeper parts of the swimming area it isn't possible to see the bottom, which gives this more of a feel of a wild swim or river swimming rather than the traditional open-air pool feeling. This extends to access into the water, which is sometimes slippery due to algae, though non-slip mats and handrails help.

This is one of those bodies of water that encourages you to reflect, and examine what you like about swimming. There is space in this lido for a peaceful, contemplative swim while others about you enjoy swimming, splashing and cooling off. After your swim spend a little time lounging on a towel by the side of the swimming area, or on top of the lido building enjoying the surroundings.

The catering available on site allows you to sit outside and admire the swimmers to one side and those out on pedalos around the lake to the other.

If planning a swim at the Serpentine you should use public transport as there are no easy or cheap places to park nearby, but there is an enjoyable walk from whichever corner of the park you come from – Lancaster Gate/Paddington, Marble Arch, South Kensington and Green Park tube stations all work broadly well if you're heading to the lido in the middle of London's most central park.

If you've invested in a day's Travelcard and want to get more swimming value from it or fancy a longer walk around the sights of London, a swim in the Serpentine would make a great public-transport lido trip combined with the Oasis near Covent Garden.

TOOTING BEC LIDO

ENGLAND London

Tooting Bec Lido
Tooting Bec Road, Tooting
London
SW16 1RU

- enquiries@tootingbeclido.co.uk
- 020 8871 7198
- placesforpeopleleisure.org/centres/tooting-bec-lido
- @tootingbeclido
- @tootingbeclido

- 91.5 m x 30 m
- Corporately run on behalf of the council
- Seasonal for non-members
- Unheated
- Freshwater
- Limited parking on site
- On-site café

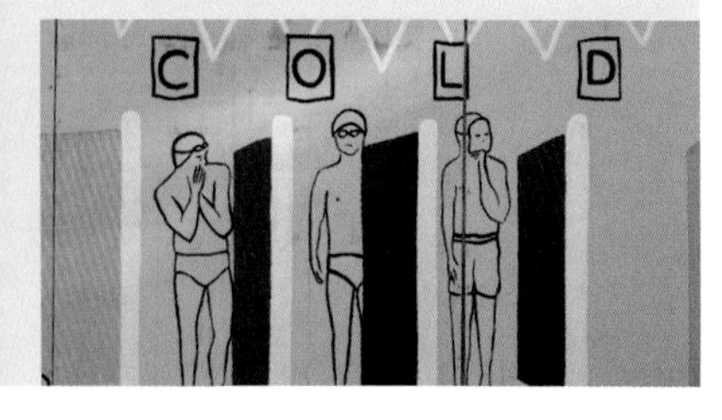

London is not short on big pools, but Tooting is the biggest of them all. It lies at the heart of the common, and the approach is green and pleasant but gives nothing away about what lies beyond the fence.

Such is the size of the pool that it will hit you full in the face as soon as you step away from the admission desk. It's hard not to gasp, or utter a muted exclamation, on your first visit. When your eyes do begin to wander from the pool itself you'll notice the brightly coloured poolside changing cubicles that are an iconic feature of Tooting Bec; you'll recognise them instantly if you have ever seen a photograph of this pool. Your gaze will move on to take in the wedding-cake fountain, the Art Deco style and the oddly contemporary circular changing blocks. They provide a haven of warmth when the weather is chilly, but even

though they have some architectural appeal of their own they do feel curiously out of keeping with the rest of the site. They do have good provision for disabled swimmers including an accessible toilet, shower and hoist.

Due to its size the pool is not quick to warm up with the onset of summer, and it can be a bit cooler than some of the other unheated pools in London. For some, however, that is part of its charm, and in winter it's a positive bonus for the South London Swimming Club members who run the site for members-only cold-water swimming. During the winter months the only real opportunity to swim if you are not an SLSC member is to enter the biannual UK cold-water swimming championships. Some swimmers take that very seriously, going all out to win medals, but there is also much to appeal to the swimmer who prefers competitions to have an emphasis on fun. The heads-up breaststroke races, featuring prizes for best hats, encourage very impressive competitive millinery and it is worth going along to spectate even if swimming in cold water isn't your bag.

The rest of the year, however, the pool is open to the general public. The water may remain a little cool, but the site is very sunny and has plenty of space for lounging about and topping up the tan. Despite its large capacity, you can expect to queue for some time if you're not there bright and early on a hot day, as this is a very popular pool when the sun beats down.

HALTWHISTLE SWIMMING AND LEISURE CENTRE

ENGLAND Northumberland

Haltwhistle Swimming and Leisure Centre
Greencroft, Haltwhistle
Northumberland
NE49 9DP

- reception@haltwhistleleisure.co.uk
- 01434 320727
- haltwhistleleisure.co.uk
- @HSLC1
- Haltwhistle Swimming and Leisure Centre
- @haltwhistleleisure

- 25 m x 10 m
- Charitable trust run
- Seasonal
- Heated
- Freshwater
- Free parking available on site
- On-site café

Even before you go for a swim at Haltwhistle, located centrally and well signposted in this small town, it is worth stopping and contemplating the claim that this is the centre of Britain. While some dispute this claim, it is worth asking whether Haltwhistle represents the central point of the lido distribution in the UK. It's not a spoiler to tell you that it isn't! It's England's most northerly pool, and we've only found six publicly accessible pools further north in Britain (although the work being done to reopen Tynemouth Outdoor Pool would make that seven!).

On the A69 and almost equidistant between Carlisle and Newcastle, this pool isn't difficult to find. Given that Haltwhistle has a population of less than 4,000 people you may be expecting to read about a small, historic, unheated pool run by volunteers, as so many in this book are. However, it isn't any of those things. It is a modern leisure centre with three heated pools (for swimming, learners and toddlers) and a gigantic flume slide set in a grassy area suitable to stay all day and picnic in. All the pools are heated to a very decent temperature, and the five-lane 25-metre pool is great for swimming, inflatable sessions and general fun days out. The changing rooms are located within the sports centre complex and there is a café here too for refreshments. Together with free parking on site this pool is something of a surprise in lots of ways, and to see it full is a delight.

Haltwhistle pool would make a lovely lido road trip taking in Helmsley and Weardale to the south, the pools of Cumbria to the west or en route to a tour of Scotland's open-air pools.

ABBEY MEADOWS OUTDOOR POOL

ENGLAND Oxfordshire

Abbey Meadows Outdoor Pool
Abbey Close, Abingdon
Oxfordshire
OX14 3JE

- abingdonoutdoorpool@gmail.com
- 01235 529321
- better.org.uk/leisure-centre/vale-of-white-horse/abbey-meadows-outdoor-pool
- @abbeyswimming
- Abbey Meadows Outdoor Pool

- L-shaped
- Corporately run on behalf of the council
- Seasonal
- Heated
- Freshwater
- Neighbouring pay-and-display car park
- None available

Abbey Meadows is a large open-air pool on the banks of the River Thames in Abingdon. The setting really is lovely, with views of moored boats and the farmland beyond. It is a heated freshwater pool in a very effective L-shaped arrangement in the middle of a grassed area, the perfect place to spend a day alternating between dips in the water and relaxing. You can swim laps up and down the side of the pool closest to the river, or swim for relaxation in the other part of the pool that has a non-slip-beach-style sloping entry.

The changing-room blocks offer single-sex communal changing rooms with one or two individual cubicles, and the whole facility has benefited from extensive refurbishment

over the winter of 2017/2018. There is a good level of disabled access, with a dedicated toilet. At time of writing there was no hoist or pool chair, but as the refurbishment was recent this may change, so do call ahead if this is essential to you. The pool has parking close by and is also within walking distance of a supermarket and the centre of town for picnic supplies if you haven't brought them with you.

Now run by Better Leisure, which operates a number of other outdoor pools in the south-east of England, this pool has been run in the past by local community volunteers, who fundraised tirelessly and kept the pool going through many previous seasons. It is definitely worth a visit, whether you are local or travelling from afar, as Abingdon has a leisurely feel to it despite its proximity to the hectic A34. You can create a day away swimming here and in nearby Hinksey Pool, in the heart of Oxford, and feel as if you've had a holiday. It would also work well for a lido road trip alongside Woodgreen in Banbury, and Riverside Park in Wallingford.

WOODGREEN LEISURE CENTRE

ENGLAND Oxfordshire

Woodgreen Leisure Centre
Woodgreen Avenue, Banbury
Oxfordshire
OX16 0HS

- woodgreen@legacyleisure.org.uk
- 01295 262742
- leisurecentre.com/woodgreen-leisure-centre
- @WoodgreenLC

- 50 m x 18 m
- Corporately run on behalf of the council
- Seasonal
- Heated
- Freshwater
- Free parking available on site
- Snack kiosk

This is an outdoor pool that has the capacity to make your heart sing. Saved from demolition, it is the kind of place that always seems to be busy and makes you wonder why it ever fell out of public use in the first place. A traditional 1930s red-brick building houses the pool, with a modern leisure centre attached, and surrounds the 50-metre, five-lane, 18-metre wide heated outdoor pool, open during the summer months and run by a leisure company. It is a great place to swim long, straight lengths or enjoy water play in the pool or on the adjacent big slide and splash areas.

© Amanda Harwood

As one would expect from a pool with modern facilities, there is good disabled access, with lifts, ramps, a hoist and dedicated changing/bathroom facilities. There are modern changing rooms (cubicles) leading to showers, and poolside there is a veranda and kiosk selling refreshments. There is space around the pool to dry off, but this isn't a lounging sort of pool – and the timetable is split into separate sessions covering the needs of all swimmers, from families to the earlier morning training-swim crowd.

Free car parking on site makes the entrance fee for a single swim all the more attractive and there are several other pools within 25 miles of Woodgreen, making this a good lido road trip pool to combine with Kenilworth to the north, Woodstock, Hinksey, Abingdon and High Wycombe to the south and Chipping Norton, Cheltenham and Cirencester to the west.

CHIPPING NORTON LIDO

ENGLAND Oxfordshire

Chipping Norton Lido
Fox Close, Chipping Norton
Oxfordshire
OX7 5BZ

- info@chippylido.co.uk
- 01608 643188
- chippylido.co.uk
- @ChippyLido
- @ChippyLido

- 25 m x 10 m
- Volunteer run
- Seasonal
- Heated
- Freshwater
- Limited parking on site; several free public car parks in town
- On-site café

Chipping Norton is worthy of an afternoon out in its own right, a lovely little town where pale stone buildings glow in the sun. That adds to the lure of this lido significantly. To find the pool you pass slightly out of the chocolate-box town centre and into a housing estate. You'll fear you've lost your way despite the clear signage urging you on. You'll emerge into a car park, at the rear of the estate, with a low-slung and unremarkable brick building that looks more like municipal football-team changing rooms than it does a lido.

You will, however, know that you're in the right place because the distinctive soundscape of an outdoor pool will rise over the walls like a gentle swell on a sandy beach. You might also glimpse a wet and excited swimmer rising above the wall as they reach the top of the slide

before launching themselves downwards into the water.

Entering through the long corridor past reception, the tiled sign will leave you in no doubt at all that you have arrived at Chippy Lido; you might even recognise it from an episode of *Top Gear* where a Rolls-Royce was driven, rock-and-roll style, into the pool. Pools are, of necessity, good at diversifying income streams, but that must be one of the most novel methods we've come across.

There are two pools on site, with a charming little café and a spacious grassy area for picnics and sunbathing. The main pool has been refurbished in recent years and has a deliciously tactile, sophisticated Hydrazzo finish with tasteful green-glass-mosaic lane lines. The Hydrazzo feels so good underfoot that you could be forgiven for standing about a while, wriggling your toes to savour it.

The aforementioned slide is one of the fastest we've ever been on, and as much as it may be slightly surreal to see a swimmer at the top from outside the walls, it is just as surreal to be that swimmer looking over the wall and into the upstairs windows of the houses across the car park. When you get to the top of the slide you'll appreciate how sheltered this site is, as any breeze blowing licks across the top of the wall to taste your wet skin; down in the belly of the site itself, the high brick walls, so unremarkable from the outside, serve to protect and cosset swimmers. The smaller pool is a giant paddling pool ideal for smaller swimmers. It isn't always uncovered if the pool isn't very busy, but ask the staff and they'll open it for you if they can.

The site is mainly level, and swimmers with reduced mobility will welcome the sturdy steps with handrails that offer easy access into the shallow end. As this book went to print the pool had invested in a hoist, which will be a welcome development for swimmers who rely on that.

HINKSEY OUTDOOR POOL

ENGLAND Oxfordshire

Hinksey Outdoor Pool
Hinksey Park, Abingdon Road, Oxford
Oxfordshire
OX1 4PZ

- hinksey@fusion-lifestyle.com
- 03448 933222
- fusion-lifestyle.com/centres/hinksey-outdoor-pool
- @HinkseyPools
- @HinkseyOutdoorPool
- @Hinksey_Outdoor_Pool

- Irregular, 33 m at widest
- Corporately run on behalf of the council
- Seasonal
- Heated
- Freshwater
- Small car park off Abingdon Road
- Snack kiosk

It is a rarity to have outdoor pools remain alive in the centre of towns where there is a strong circular relationship between development and property prices. The temptation for local authorities is, all too often, to divest themselves of an asset that they aren't maximising after years of underinvestment in order to sell on the site and reap future rewards from council tax levied on the homes that are inevitably built. We are beyond grateful that Hinksey hasn't been levelled under a developer's bulldozer, because it is a wonderful pool set in spacious and well-tended grounds.

This pool lends itself very well to arriving by public transport, lying just ten minutes' level walk from the dead centre of Oxford; as parking is incredibly limited, and much of central Oxford is closed to traffic, you may find bringing the car to be a positive disadvantage. If you have reduced mobility a taxi from the train station or bus station will not break the bank, but there will still be a walk of a minute or two from where the taxi can drop you off, so be prepared for that. That walk will be no shorter if you are lucky enough to secure one of the small number of disabled parking spaces in the car park. Once at the pool, however, you will find it equipped with a dedicated disabled toilet and changing facility, and there is a pool chair that can be used to wheel a swimmer into deep water via the beach-style sloping entry.

The pool is large, and roughly figure-of-eight shaped. One side of the pool is deeper and is predominantly used by those looking for uninterrupted lengths. The other side features the shallow, beach-style entry that offers ease of access as well as being appealing to families and those who want to wallow in the water and soak up the sun. The two pools meet at the neck of the eight, and a lane rope stops swimmers drifting from one side to the other. There are traditional, well-maintained red-and-white poolside changing cubicles and the grassy areas are a pleasure to spread out a towel or picnic rug on and snooze away the afternoon post-swim.

The pool also offers some special events, such as night swimming, which are well attended and need fast booking in advance if you're not to miss out. Oxford is, deservedly, a very popular destination for tourists of all stripes, and Hinksey should definitely feature in your lido tourism plans.

RIVERSIDE PARK AND POOLS

ENGLAND Oxfordshire

Riverside Park and Pools
Crowmarsh Gifford, Wallingford
Oxfordshire
OX10 8EB

- Via contact form on website
- 020 3859 8208
- better.org.uk/leisure-centre/south-oxfordshire/riverside-park-and-pools
- @Better_UK
- Riverside Park and Pools

- 23 m x 10 m
- Corporately run on behalf of the council
- Seasonal
- Heated
- Freshwater
- Parking available on site
- Snack kiosk

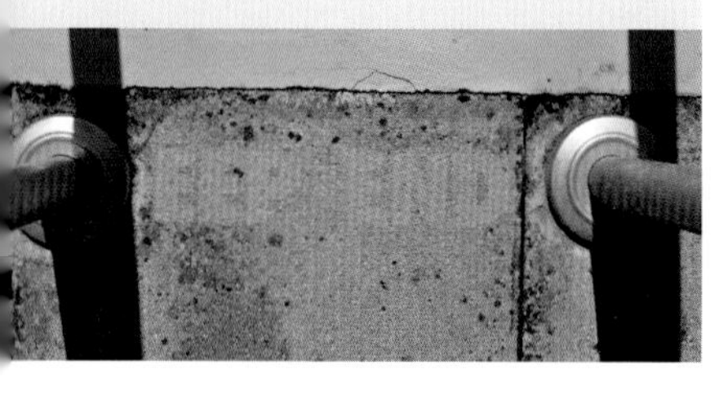

The sparkling blue heated water of Riverside pool is delightful to swim in whatever the weather. The pool's bright water with the river and pretty town of Wallingford beyond is tailor-made for your Instagram feed.

This heated, seasonal outdoor pool sits in a large campsite and park next to the River Thames. At 23 metres long and three lanes wide, it is one of those pools that you can see, and anticipate swimming in, from the moment you make the rather sharp turning from the main road by Wallingford Bridge to the campsite and gently drive down the track towards the large car park adjacent to the pool. The changing rooms and toilets are in a building at one end of the pool, where the reception desk and snack kiosk are also housed.

The pool is surrounded by enough space to sit and while

away a few hours, but since this pool benefits from both an adjacent park and a free-to-use children's splash pad you might be tempted to explore those after your swim. It is also within walking distance from the centre of town if you're inclined to round off your visit with browsing the shops and cafés. This is one of several riverside outdoor pools in the UK (others include Beccles, Abingdon, Lazonby, Ingleton and Chagford). There is something about swimming in a riverside pool that makes one feel even more connected to the natural environment, and makes you feel grateful that someone had the foresight to build a pool here and decide to warm the water up a little! If you have experience of swimming in rivers you might like to consider having a dip in the Thames. There is a good, shallow access point on the same bank but on the other side of the bridge. Do take care to watch out for boat traffic.

There is good provision for disabled swimmers at this pool, including a hoist for access into the water.

WOODSTOCK OPEN AIR POOL

ENGLAND Oxfordshire

Woodstock Open Air Pool
Shipton Road, Woodstock
Oxfordshire
OX20 1LW

- Via contact form on website
- 01993 811785
- better.org.uk/leisure-centre/west-oxfordshire/woodstock-open-air-pool
- @Better_UK
- Woodstock Open Air Pool

- 25 m x 10 m
- Corporately run on behalf of the council
- Seasonal
- Heated
- Freshwater
- Parking available on site
- Snack kiosk

Woodstock Open Air Pool has little to commend it architecturally, being fronted by a plain white brick of a building sandwiched between a large school and a car park. Don't be deterred by that, however; not all lidos can have the visual appeal of the historic pools like Tinside, Peterborough et al. The workaday buildings contain decent changing facilities, including a dedicated disabled changing area with its own shower, and as you emerge blinking into the light you'll be met by an ample pool with a diving board that you may well be allowed to use if the pool isn't busy. There are sloping steps

with a handrail to ease access into the pool, but no hoist.

The water is heated, the tiled pool is well maintained and the grounds are big enough for some serious loafing about if the sun shines. The snack kiosk is not always open, but that isn't a drawback as this isn't a pool where you can stay all day. It closes entirely in between timed sessions, so plan in advance if you don't want to be eating your picnic in the car park while you wait for the pool to reopen. And yes, that is the voice of personal experience – part of the research for this book has involved eating the mistimed picnics so you don't have to.

ALBRIGHTON SWIMMING POOL

ENGLAND Shropshire

Albrighton Swimming Pool
Albrighton Primary School, Newhouse Lane, Albrighton
Shropshire
WV7 3QS

- committee@albrightonswimclub.onmicrosoft.com
- None
- albrightonswimming.co.uk
- @Albrighton_Swim
- facebook.com/AlbrightonSwimmingClub
- @adswimclub

- 15 m x 7.5 m
- Community run
- Seasonal
- Heated
- Freshwater
- Parking available on site
- Snack kiosk

Albrighton is a little known, but very fine, example of a council-run pool sited on school property that volunteers have stepped in to save from closure. The pool is now run, on behalf of the community, by Albrighton & District Swimming Club.

Volunteers taking on school pools is a rising trend and others, such as at Overton in Hampshire where (at the time of writing) Lordsfield Swimming Club were making every effort to negotiate a lease with the council, will no doubt be joining the fold with the rise of academy trusts and ever-increasing pressure on public-sector budgets.

The practical dynamics of running a voluntary effort within the constraints of council leases and an in-school location can't be underestimated, and Albrighton SC do a marvelous job. The pool is impeccably maintained, as are the part-grassy, part-paved grounds it sits in. There are indoor changing areas, including accessible areas; the Braille signage is a welcome addition not often seen at pools.

Access onto the site is level, as is the paved area around the pool. Access into the tank is via ladders. The paved area includes a large patio, and there are plenty of chairs. The gently sloping grassy banks offer shady spots to sit with a picnic, although Albrighton itself is a handsome little town with plenty of lunch options if you fancy a treat above and beyond your sandwiches and the offerings from the kiosk. The young, and young at heart, will be thrilled to see the baskets of woggles and floats, and there are water-polo nets to add to the fun.

This pool is approached around a corner, and the brick-wall-dominated approach gives away little of the blue-green oasis that lies beyond. It's a relatively small site, so on brilliant summer days this is a pool that is likely to be busy and you will need to be prepared to queue.

SEVERN CENTRE OUTDOOR POOL

ENGLAND Shropshire

Severn Centre Outdoor Pool
Severn Centre, Bridgnorth Road, Highley
Shropshire
WV16 6JG

- info@severncentre.co.uk
- 01746 860000
- haloleisure.org.uk/centres/shropshire/severn-centre
- @SevernCentre
- Severn Centre
- @severn.centre

- 25 m x 10 m
- Corporately run on behalf of the council
- Seasonal
- Heated
- Freshwater
- Parking available on site
- On-site café

When visiting the Severn Centre in Highley it is, excitingly, possible to arrive by steam train along the Severn Valley Railway from either Bridgnorth (and its steep Cliff Railway) or Kidderminster, alighting at Highley station. You will need to time your visit to the pool alongside the times of the trains and enjoy a brisk walk uphill from the station to the pool – it isn't one of those days that you could leave to chance and hope to catch a train easily in either direction *and* swim without planning it first. But the effort taken to plan this will be well worth it.

Highley is a standard 25-metre long pool set in lovely, rural surroundings. It has spacious communal changing rooms, and its position at the top of the hill lends a 'big sky' feel to it that is so loved by those who swim outside. It sits alongside a building that is an important hub for the community. It houses the usual facilities one would expect to find in a leisure centre but, importantly, it also houses the library. Many community-run outdoor pools offer small, informal lending libraries poolside, but Highley definitely raises the bar.

While the pool has car parking right outside the front door, level or ramped access and disabled-accessible toilet/changing facilities, the only access to the tank is via vertical ladders.

As it is set in a former mining village, there is plenty to reflect on during a visit to this pool about the importance of local resources for local people and those who maintain heritage resources for the enjoyment of others.

CLEVEDON MARINE LAKE

ENGLAND Somerset

Clevedon Marine Lake
170 Old Church Road, Clevedon
Somerset
BS21 7TU

- info@clevedonmarinelake.co.uk
- 01275 877180
- clevedonmarinelake.co.uk
- @clevedonlake
- @clevedonlake
- @clevedonlake

- 15,000 sq m
- Volunteer run
- Year round
- Unheated
- Saltwater
- Nearby car park and on-street parking
- None available

Tidal pools are a powerful reminder of humanity's fragility in the face of nature, and the ingenuity with which that fragility is overcome. Like many of its ilk, Clevedon Marine Lake was built in the Victorian era when feats of engineering were something of a status symbol for a town, and when coastal areas were keen to capitalise on the fashion for taking the sea air as a curative tonic no longer reserved solely for the upper classes.

The lake is big, some 250 metres long along the sea wall, and it is a very effective way of damming the huge tidal range of the Bristol Channel. It is the second largest tidal range in the world, and that makes swimming in the sea a potentially dangerous proposition if you are not familiar with the local currents. The lake is, therefore, a truly safe haven that makes swimming achievable at any time of the day and year.

In recent years the marine lake has been extensively refurbished, and is now regularly desilted to maintain its depth. There is ample hard standing for sunbathing and/or changing, and a small slipway for dinghies and kayaks. Swimmers tend to congregate at the opposite end of the lake to the slipway, tucked under the cliffs below Poets' Walk where there are steps with handrails in and out of the water, as well as ramped access down to poolside. There is a good-sized pay and display car

park at Salthouse Fields, and the Salthouse pub is very welcoming of swimmers. In winter that is particularly useful as there are no covered facilities at all at the lake itself, and no café or snack kiosk, so a post-swim hot chocolate indoors is very welcome when the weather is poor.

While small watercraft do use the lake, it is predominantly home to a very active and very welcoming group of swimmers. You will find somebody in the water most days, right through the year. The infinity-pool view up to Clevedon Pier is worth the swim alone. The pool isn't lifeguarded at any time of year, and it is best to avoid swimming here when rough weather and big tides that overtop the sea wall combine. Even when gentle seas wash over the sea wall some care is needed, and you should avoid the area alongside the wall as getting swept over and out to sea is a serious proposition given the strength of the tide. There are no changing facilities, so al fresco changing skills are required, as is a weather eye on your kit; it will get wet and/or washed away if you leave it on the ground when the tide comes in.

GREENBANK SWIMMING POOL

ENGLAND Somerset

Greenbank Swimming Pool
Wilfrid Road, Street
Somerset
BA16 OEU

- info@greenbankpool.co.uk
- 01458 442468
- greenbankpool.co.uk
- @greenbank_pool
- @GreenbankPool
- @greenbank_swimming_pool

- 30 m x 12 m
- Charitable trust run
- Seasonal
- Heated
- Freshwater
- Parking available at Greenbank Pool car park or within walking distance at other local car parks
- Snack kiosk

Like several other lidos in this book, Greenbank was built for the town as an act of benevolence; in this case the benefactors were the Clark family, who established the still thriving shoe business in this small Somerset town.

The lido is, like much of the housing also provided for the workers by the family, pretty and individual. Whereas the housing is quaintly built of rough-hewn local stone, the pool is an understated Art Deco gem. Its crisp, white-rendered façade offers a tantalising glimpse of what lies beyond as you approach reception, as does a stroll down the high street, where chain-link fencing allows an open view of the pools and the gardens that surround them.

After the turnstiles the site falls away down grassy banking and wide, shallow steps to the semicircular toddler pool. Beyond that lies the main tank, all ringed by low walls containing the paved poolside areas. The walls mark a boundary between paving and grass, with a lot of space for picnicking. An unusual feature of this pool is that a local café will deliver food to the pool if you place a telephone order. Rendezvous café's website was showing as under redevelopment when this book went to print, so if you are planning on ordering your lunch in you should phone ahead and check. The café's website is linked to via the pool's website, under the 'shop' section.

One corner of the site is home to a large splash pad, wet play area with slide, fountains and jets that are terrific fun for children and the young at heart. There is also a small play area with swings, and an indoor games room where young people often congregate. There are some fairly basic covered-over changing areas and toilets, but most visitors to Greenbank seem to favour the old-school approach of changing under towels on the grass.

On hot days Greenbank is a magnet for visitors from a wide geographic area, and you will find it to be very busy with long queues. There is little in the way of public transport, so most visitors will come by car, and there is very limited parking outside the pool. You can, as an alternative, pay to park in the extensive car parks at Clarks Village retail complex and walk through to the high street to find the pool. There is free on-street parking available in the town, but when the pool is busy you are likely to be parked a fifteen-minute walk away at least, as much of the surrounding area is restricted for the benefit of residents. You'll have none of these issues on more overcast days, however, and this is a pool that is definitely worth a bit of hassle.

The steps and transitions between slabs and grass that are a feature of this pool may make it a challenging location for wheelchair users. There is level access from the rear of the site, and it will be worth calling ahead to make sure that can be opened for you if you plan on visiting with a wheelchair. You need to cross grass to access the paved routes to the building, but there is accessible changing provision with a sit-down shower. There is no hoist, and only one disabled parking space outside the pool.

PORTISHEAD OPEN AIR POOL

ENGLAND Somerset

Portishead Open Air Pool
Esplanade Road, Portishead
Somerset
BS20 7HD

- info@portisheadopenairpool.org.uk, manager@portisheadopenairpool.org.uk
- 01275 843454
- portisheadopenairpool.org.uk
- @PortisheadLido
- @PortisheadOpenAirPool
- @portisheadlido

- 33 m x 17 m
- Volunteer run
- Seasonal, but open off season unheated
- Heated
- Freshwater
- Free on-street parking
- On-site café

Pledger pic: *Sophie Pusill*

Portishead lies on the very edge of the Bristol Channel, the enormous tidal range practically lapping at the pool's exterior wall. The pool and adjoining café is community run by a team of volunteers, and the café makes the best of the water's-edge location, with views across to the Welsh hills. It also makes the best of some very talented local bakers, serving home-made cakes that are as mouth-watering as they are beautiful. The estuary views are not visible from poolside, thanks to the sturdy stone wall that keeps the worst of the sea breezes at bay, but climbing to the top of the extensive sun terraces will deliver a view that is hard to beat. If you are lucky you may see huge ships pass close by as they hug the deep-water channel into

Avonmouth. The view at sunset, early and late in the season, is particularly worth the climb.

Built in the early 1960s, concrete is, as you would expect, used to impressive effect at Portishead; its architecture was thoroughly modern when built and it made the most of the steeply sloping, south-facing site. The terraces are broad, wide steps that are in full sun all day. Visitors will need to bear that in mind on hot days, as there is very little natural shade. The concrete diving boards, long since out of use due to changing health and safety regulations, have an elegant, angular line. They are starkly beautiful in their simplicity from whichever angle one views them, and are an iconic feature of this very individual and colourful pool.

The boards tower over the deep end of a 33-metre tank that has been recently refurbished, and in the summer months the water is heated, while in winter months cold-water swimming is on offer. Underwater lighting was installed in the main pool as part of the refurbishment, and that contributes to an extensive programme of special events such as full-moon swims. A small baby pool lies at the bottom of the terraces, and visitors can ask for it to be filled on request; sun hats to shade little faces will be a good idea.

This is a pool that delivers a 'wow' factor to first-time visitors, but also inspires passion and commitment on the part of regular swimmers and the volunteers that run it. You'll feel that sense of community when you visit, so do plan in some time to stop and chat. Portishead also lies just five minutes off the M5 near Bristol, so if you are a swimmer beating a path south or north, you will find this to be an ideal place to break your journey, and much nicer than Gordano services.

There is level access all around the pool, apart from the terraces, and dedicated wet-room changing facilities for disabled swimmers. There is no hoist, but there are gently sloping steps with good handrails providing access to the shallow end.

SHEPTON MALLET LIDO

ENGLAND Somerset

Shepton Mallet Lido
Shaftgate Avenue, Shepton Mallet
Somerset
BA4 5YA

- shepton-sales@fusion-lifestyle.com
- 01749 347851
- fusion-lifestyle.com/centres/shepton-mallet-lido
- @sheptonlido
- @sheptonlido
- @shepton_mallet_lido

- 25 m x 10 m
- Corporately run on behalf of the council
- Seasonal
- Heated
- Freshwater
- Parking available on site
- Snack kiosk

If you have heard of Shepton Mallet at all it is likely to be as a result of Glastonbury Festival, which takes place close by (closer to Shepton Mallet, in fact, than to Glastonbury), or cider. This is the heart of cider and perry country, with commercial cider producers still much in evidence in the town. One of Shepton Mallet Lido's quirks is that, until very recently, when new boilers were installed, the pool was heated by hot water that was the by-product of the neighbouring cider producer.

Those neighbours give the view over the wall that runs alongside the pool a somewhat industrial feel, but that doesn't spoil what is otherwise a lovely facility. It's tricky to find, but is signposted off the main road and your satnav will take you very nearly to the door – provided you trust it as you turn into a housing estate that looks an unlikely home for a lido. You may also miss the pool as you drive past, but if you look out for a small car park with a portacabin-type building at the far side you'll have found your mark and will then notice the sign above the door.

On hot days this pool reaches capacity quickly, as it is a relatively small site, but at

other times you are likely to be untroubled by crowds. It's not a high-profile pool, and it is not easy to get to by public transport; those things both play a role in it being uncrowded. It deserves to be a good deal busier, however, and we hope it will be.

As well as the main 25-metre pool there is also a smaller pool for children or less-confident swimmers, as well as a splash pad that is ideally suited to toddlers. There is a sunny grassed area and picnic tables, as well as a nicely stocked kiosk to take the edge off a swimmer's appetite. The operator has invested a decent sum in overhauling this pool in recent years, but not at the expense of its charm. It doesn't feel bland and corporate, the changing rooms retain a traditionally basic feel and there truly is something here to suit swimmers of all ages and abilities. It is a lido that punches above its weight in terms of what it has to offer. And if you plan it right it will make for a great double-dip lido road trip with Greenbank in Street.

There are steps on site, which can be avoided by the use of ramps. Access into the pool is by ladders.

TINTINHULL VILLAGE SWIMMING POOL

ENGLAND Somerset

Tintinhull Village Swimming Pool
Tintinhull, Yeovil
Somerset
BA22 8PW

- tintinhullpool@gmail.com
- None
- tintinhull.net/amenities/pool

- 25 m x 6 m
- Volunteer run
- Seasonal
- Heated
- Freshwater
- Car parks available next to the village hall and opposite the church
- None available

Tintinhull is a pool in stealth mode; it gives the impression of not much needing, or wanting, huge crowds of visitors. Which is not to say that it is an unfriendly place – far from it. When we visited we were warmly greeted by the volunteers on duty, and we had a lovely long chat with them, but it was also clear that not many lido road trippers make it to Tintinhull. It is such a low-profile pool that despite both of us living an hour's drive from it, and having spent years actively looking for lidos, this was one of the last publicly accessible pools to come to our attention. And we stumbled on it by accident, almost, when the then-manager of Portishead Open Air Pool sent us a link to a blog that mentioned it. Within a matter of hours we were in the car, off in search of it.

It is not a huge pool, being only three lanes or so wide, but it is a full 25 metres in length. It sits in the centre of Tintinhull, at the far side of the smallish recreation ground/play area. You'll need to make a turn off the main road that runs through the village, and be careful to park considerately of residents' driveways when you find it.

We were charmed by Tintinhull. It has very rustic timber communal changing rooms and a breeze-block toilet outhouse, with few other facilities, but there is space for lounging about and the water is delightfully warm. The pool does not have its own website, but features on a site that lists all the village amenities, so you'll need to make sure you are on the right page to check the opening times. It is staffed by volunteers, and is not lifeguarded. If there are no volunteers signed up for a particular session it will not open, so a degree of flexibility is needed if you're planning to come any distance to swim here.

Swimmers with limited mobility will also need to note that to get to the pool you need to walk across uneven grass for a few minutes, and that there are no dedicated toilet or changing facilities for disabled swimmers. Access into the pool is via ladders.

WIVEY POOL

ENGLAND Somerset

Wivey Pool
The Recreation Ground, Wiveliscombe
Somerset
TA4 2TA

- wiveypool@gmail.com
- 01984 624720
- wiveypool.net
- @wiveypool
- @wiveypoolofficial

- 25 m x 10 m
- Volunteer run
- Seasonal
- Heated
- Freshwater
- Car parks next to pool and opposite recreation ground, and on-street parking on Croft Way
- Snack kiosk

Wiveliscombe will take a little effort, nestled as it is in the heart of the Somerset countryside, well off the beaten track. But it will be all the more worth it for that.

There is every chance that when you visit you will be driving; public transport out here is thin on the ground. There is also every chance that you will miss the pool at your first attempt, as the postcode will take you to a spot nearly 50 metres up the road. Your landmark should be the handsome recreation ground, which you will not be able to miss; you may just catch a glimpse of the pool cover above the fence if the pool is open. At the right-hand end of the recreation ground, as you look at it from the road, there is a small unsignposted turning in front of a house that sits at right angles to the road. Take this turning to a small car park;

if it is full you will have to take your chances on the road, but at least you will know where you are going if you have to park elsewhere and approach on foot.

From the car park you are looking at the end of the perimeter wall. Follow it to your left, towards the recreation ground, and you will see the gate just as you round the corner. Once inside, you can sign in and pay your admission money.

Wivey Pool packs a lot into a small space, including a huge amount of creativity and community spirit. There is often some sort of community challenge on to engage swimmers, and the blackboards give a real sense of the spirit and enthusiasm that goes into them. The site is dominated by the 25-metre pool, accessed via ladders, flanked by somewhat agricultural wooden buildings. We say that with not a hint of criticism. This is a countryside pool, and the timber buildings with stable doors perfectly marry with that. It would be hard to imagine anything else working better here. The changing rooms are basic but functional, although the addition of some dedicated space for disabled swimmers could be useful. There are some snacks and hot drinks available from the kiosk that operates from the office, should you feel that you are wasting away during your visit.

There is a small amount of space for sunbathing, but as this pool opens for defined sessions you aren't likely to have planned to stay all day. If you do, you can decamp to the recreation ground, enjoy a picnic and the play area, and be right on hand when the pool reopens in the afternoon. Wivey Pool is an excellent example of a much-loved community pool.

BECCLES LIDO

ENGLAND Suffolk

Beccles Lido
Puddingmoor, Beccles
Suffolk
NR34 9PL

- info@beccleslido.com
- 01502 713297
- beccleslido.com
- @BecclesLido
- @beccleslido

- 33 m x 17 m
- Volunteer run
- Seasonal
- Heated
- Freshwater
- On-street parking
- Snack kiosk

Beccles Lido is one of only two open-air swimming pools in Suffolk (and there are no longer any at all in Norfolk), although it would make a great lido road trip to combine a swim here with Brightlingsea Lido in Essex if you were heading to East Anglia.

Its riverside setting is the perfect place for a large, heated lido. Parking outside is limited and the pool is a decent but doable walk from Beccles town centre. Once you are here, it has the feel of a place that you'd like to not only spend a good amount of time in but also want to revisit.

The original changing rooms for this 33-metre lido are poolside cubicles with large wooden doors that run alongside the shallow end of the pool together with lockers and showers. They are charming, and it's lovely that they were retained when the more modern changing and toilet block was installed at the far end of the site. The pool borders the river along the deep end and there are trees along the length of the pool

opposite the changing rooms, providing shady places to lounge on the grass or on one of the many loungers around the pool on warm days.

Beccles is well equipped for adventurous visitors, with a slide, diving board and inflatable sessions. It also offers more serene lane-swimming sessions, however; something for everyone. The site is level, with ramps where necessary, and there are dedicated disabled changing facilities and a hoist to access the water.

One of the great joys of Beccles Lido is that it was saved and bought from the district council by those who wanted to retain the pool on behalf of the town. Over the last few years extensive fundraising, combined with the will and determination of volunteers and local swimmers as well as visitors, has not only made this pool a going concern over the summer months but also helped to raise sufficient money to invest in its development for the future. With some strong parallels with Buckfastleigh Open Air Pool in this regard, the work that volunteers have done here at Beccles Lido is to be admired as much as the swimming pool is to be enjoyed and revelled in, whatever the weather.

BROOMHILL POOL

ENGLAND Suffolk

HISTORIC POOLS OF BRITAIN

Broomhill Pool
Sherrington Road, Ipswich
Suffolk
IP1 4HT

- info@savebroomhillpool.org
- None
- savebroomhillpool.org
- @broomhillpool
- @broomhillpooltrust

- 50 m x 18 m
- Corporately run on behalf of the council
- To be confirmed
- To be confirmed
- Freshwater
- On-street parking
- To be confirmed

Broomhill Pool is a glorious, Art Deco lido that, at the time the guide was written, had secured the funding needed to be restored and reopened after lying fallow for many years. The tireless work of the Save Broomhill Pool trust has resulted in a significant victory, and a much welcomed one at that.

The expected opening date is likely to be in 2020, so we aren't in a position to give a detailed description of the facility, but you can expect the Wicksteed diving platforms, once so common but now a real rarity, to be retained and restored and the overall restoration is bound to be to the same high standard that we have seen from Fusion at other pools, such as Hillingdon in Uxbridge. We also expect there to be good provision for making this pool accessible to disabled swimmers.

Keep a close eye on this project, and swim there at the first available opportunity – we certainly will!

GREAT CORNARD SPORTS CENTRE

ENGLAND Suffolk

Great Cornard Sports Centre
Head Lane, Great Cornard, Sudbury
Suffolk
CO10 0JU

- newlife@tgschool.net
- 01787 374861
- gcsportscentre.info
- Great Cornard Sports Centre

- 25 m x 10 m
- Council run
- Seasonal
- Heated
- Freshwater
- Free parking available on site
- On-site café

Great Cornard required some careful planning to get there during opening hours. This is first and foremost a school resource which is open to the public for swimming for ninety minutes a day during a ten-week period between the beginning of June and the middle of August. We calculate that of all the pools in this book, it may be open for the fewest minutes per season, with a mere 6,300 minutes of public access annually.

So, if you'd like to swim in this delightful, heated, community pool with friendly staff and lifeguards, you need to plan your arrival carefully. You also need to be aware that the pool is largely aimed at getting children to swim and enjoy the water, and that the opportunities for a brisk 1-kilometre swim up and down will be limited. The shrieks and laughter of young pool users, on a warm sunny day, are the

© Dan Lawrence

soundtrack of enjoyment.

You will need to either live locally or be a true lido enthusiast to put Great Cornard on your list of places to swim, but the place is lovely, there are clean communal changing rooms with good showers, a coffee shop and, like the Severn Centre, even the village's library is on site. You'll get a warm welcome, and it is a pool that will make you wonder which of the children swimming on the day you visit will be open-air swimming enthusiasts in the future because they learned to swim here.

If you are swimming at Great Cornard you might also want to consider a side trip to Stour Valley School (www.stourvalley-communityschool.org). This has a heated pool which, during the summer holidays, is run by Clare Swimming Club (www.facebook.com/clareswimmingpool). Casual swimmers are welcome, at very reasonable rates. It came to our attention just a couple of days before it closed for the 2018 season, so we had no chance to visit it ourselves. It's on our list for 2019!

© Dan Lawrence

© Dan Lawrence

GUILDFORD LIDO

ENGLAND Surrey

Guildford Lido
Stoke Road, Guildford
Surrey
GU1 1HB

- info@guildfordlido.co.uk
- 01483 449108
- freedom-leisure.co.uk/centres/guildford-lido
- @guildfordlido
- @guildfordlido
- @guildford_lido

- 50 m x 20 m
- Corporately run behalf of the council
- Seasonal, but open off season unheated
- Heated
- Freshwater
- Free parking available on site and at nearby Guildford Spectrum
- Snack kiosk

Guildford blends history and modernity seamlessly. One of the first things you'll see, if you're looking out for it, is the former pool attendant's house standing just outside the grounds. What a job that would have been, especially with benefits including a handsome house and a commute of just thirty seconds!

The entranceway, through a high brick arch, feels airy and contemporary, and as you walk in you are treated to a slice of the view. And it is just a slice; this pool is big, as are the grounds it lies in. It's a tantalising thing though, this sliver of view as you approach. You'll see the sun bouncing off the water, if you're lucky enough to have it, and hear the swimmers' joyful noises. You'd need to be made of very stern stuff not to feel the heart quicken a little.

Once you're inside, the scale of the place will be apparent. The history is preserved in the poolside changing areas, which are sweetly faithful to the 1930s origins of this pool – especially when seen against the smart, tiled tank, looking for all the world like it was built very recently. It won't have looked like that when the pool attendant's house was occupied, but this is the kind of modernisation that none of us can complain about. The same can be said, we imagine, for the water slides. You'll need to pay a little extra if you plan to use them, so do mention that at reception when you pay for your admission, but they are definitely worth

© Roger Taylor

the investment for the young and young at heart. The very young are also catered for, with a paddling pool and a mini-slide.

The main pool itself is big enough to cater for most needs, with tiled steps and a handrail accessing the shallow end, and there are usually lanes in. Access all around the site is level, with dedicated disabled toilet and changing facilities and a hoist to access the pool. One of Guildford's unique features is its policy of maintaining the temperature at 10°C during the winter months, when it opens for cold-water swimming on a restricted timetable. This makes it an ideal winter pool for those who like the zing of a cold swim, but who don't like the finger-pinching bite of single-figure temperatures.

ARUNDEL LIDO

ENGLAND Sussex

Arundel Lido
Queen Street, Arundel
Sussex
BN18 9JG

- manager@arundel-lido.com
- 01903 884772
- arundel-lido.com
- @ArundelLido
- @ArundelLido

- 25 m x 10 m
- Volunteer run
- Seasonal
- Heated
- Freshwater
- Pay and display car park on site
- On-site café

Some outdoor pools hide their light under a bushel; they are tucked away behind walls, fences or established swathes of greenery. You almost feel as though you have stumbled on a secret. Some pools, however, flaunt their wares for all to see. Your heart quickens as you approach, the blanket of blue throwing itself into ever sharper focus as you draw near. Arundel is one such pool, and your sense of anticipation will gradually build as you close on it.

The pool is a short stroll from the centre of this small town with its historic castle that dominates the view as you plough up and down the pool (the only pool in the UK that we're aware of where a genuine castle will fill your field of vision as you swim!). Supplementing the heated 25-metre pool is a smaller pool for little ones, and this family-friendly environment makes it the kind of pool where you want to stay for several hours, alternating between swimming and sitting on the grass or at the picnic tables with refreshments (available from the on-site café).

The site is level, and has steps with a handrail to access the pool. There is a dedicated disabled toilet and changing facilities can be made available if you ask staff. There's a hoist, and the staff prefer a call in advance so they can make sure it is ready for use.

Just off the A27, it's easy to get to, and with pay and display parking next to the pool, this is a lovely swim in the summer that could be combined with a visit to other pools (Petersfield, Saltdean, Hilsea) within a 25-mile radius for a lovely lido road trip.

BURGESS HILL LIDO

ENGLAND Sussex

Burgess Hill Lido
The Triangle Leisure Centre, Triangle Way, Burgess Hill
Sussex
RH15 8WA

- enquiries@thetriangleleisurecentre.org
- 01444 876000
- placesforpeopleleisure.org/centres/the-triangle
- @thetrianglelc
- @triangleleisurecentre
- @triangle_leisure_centre

- Irregular
- Corporately run on behalf of the council
- Seasonal
- Heated
- Freshwater
- Free parking available on site
- On-site café

Just off the M23, this is a very straightforward open-air pool to find, and with a large number of free car parking spaces outside the Triangle Leisure Centre and friendly staff on reception, there is an altogether pleasant feel to an outdoor swim here – even if there is no sense from the outside of the large (and, not surprisingly, triangular shaped) building that there is an outdoor pool beyond.

In fact, you don't get a sense of where the outdoor pool is until you have changed in the modern cubicles that form the large and busy changing village, seen the standard indoor 25-metre pool to one side and the fun pool and observed the many slides and chutes for children of all ages to the other side that you see a door leading to the outdoor pool.

The pool shelters behind high walls, with sunloungers to help you make the most of this suntrap. The lifeguard, swaddled in a thick coat on less than balmy summer days, looks out over an irregularly shaped pool from their high chair. Your first thought might be, 'Yes, but can I actually swim in this?' Irregularly shaped pools tend to suggest a paddle rather than a decent swim up and down. If you want to do laps in this heated pool you will need to pick the longest direct points between the two ends, about 20 metres apart, but the water is certainly deep enough to swim in and you can have an enjoyable outdoor swim.

Burgess Hill Lido is very much part of the Triangle Leisure Centre, rather than an afterthought. You can wander freely between the indoor pools, with their slides and chutes, and the outdoor pool with its lazy river. This means that the scope of activity on offer is likely to keep you occupied for a lot longer than you might have originally planned, particularly if you have children with you – tearing them away may prove difficult.

There's a small café and vending machines on site for a post-swim drink and snacks and there's also a shop selling things you may have forgotten to bring with you. Altogether this is an outdoor swim that doesn't evoke any sense of the lidos of yesteryear, but one where it does feel that an outdoor pool can really be part of a leisure centre offering if there's the space and the will to make it happen.

As you'd expect from a modern facility such as this there is good accessibility provision, and disabled swimmers could visit confidently expecting their needs to be met.

FINDON SWIMMING POOL

ENGLAND Sussex

Findon Swimming Pool
St John the Baptist Primary School,
School Hill, Findon Village
Sussex
BN14 0TR

- None
- 07795 578723
- findonswimmingpool.co.uk
- @FindonPool
- @FindonVillageSwimmingPool

- 15 m x 6 m
- Volunteer run
- Seasonal
- Heated
- Freshwater
- School car park available for public use at weekends and during school holidays
- Snack kiosk

Findon Swimming Pool is truly a community resource – found at the local primary school in the centre of the village and run by volunteers for the good of the other members of the community, it is well used by those who live locally.

It is a heated 15-metre pool with a slide, and there are grassy banks that surround it for sitting in the sun. Why do you, therefore, detect a note of caution in the writing about this pool? It is there for very a very good reason – this pool is open for precisely

one hour per day (3.30–4.30) on weekdays and Saturdays between May and September and, as a result, you've really got to time your journey to arrive at the pool in time for a swim.

As outdoor swims go this is a very reasonably priced one for both children and adults. However, if you swim as an adult, you might find that you are the only one – there may be lots of mums, dads and grandparents sitting on the grass supporting their swimming children, but it is not a pool that attracts a lot of adult swimmers. It has a constant depth, is heated and is surrounded by lots of colourful water-related images and painted beach huts. It isn't lifeguarded, but there will be a first-aid trained supervisor on duty for every session. If no volunteer supervisor can be found, the pool remains closed. The welcome is warm, the parking on site or on nearby roads is easy, and you can enjoy an ice cream afterwards from the kiosk. We will say again, however, that you've got to be very sure that the pool will be open on the day you want to visit by calling ahead to check. Disabled swimmers will also want to phone to discuss whether any particular needs can be met.

PELLS POOL

ENGLAND Sussex

Pells Pool
Brook Street, Lewes
Sussex
BN7 2BA

- thepellspool@yahoo.co.uk
- 01273 472334
- pellspool.org.uk
- @PellsPool
- @PellsPoolLewes
- @pellspool

- 46 m x 23 m
- Volunteer run
- Seasonal
- Unheated
- Freshwater
- Car parks at Spring Gardens and Brook Street
- Snack kiosk

Pells Pool holds a record that it can be confident will never be beaten. It is the oldest continually operating lido in the UK. Cleveland Pools is older, but has been far from continuously operated as a swimming pool. And if Pells's place in history doesn't entice you to take a lido road trip, there is much else that will.

It is a handsome pool, filled with soft, silky water

drawn direct from a spring. The timeline of the pool is written in layers all over the fabric of the place. The three-dimensional, painted stone

© Rob Read

signage at the entrance, proudly commemorating the centenary of the pool's opening in 1860, is both unique and charming. Pells is an old lady not coy about her age. The long, flint perimeter wall that runs down one side of the pool is a thing of beauty in itself. We challenge you not to reach out and trail your fingers over its textures as you walk the length of the pool to the changing rooms at the far end. These are of a younger vintage, and partly open to the elements. One gets the impression that they are the merest passing nod to modesty. Pells feels like the sort of place where getting changed under a towel, while standing on a picnic blanket spread out under the trees, is more in keeping with the traditions of swimmers now long gone.

There is a ramp, with handrails, into the shallow end, level access (with ramps where necessary around the site), a wheelchair available to borrow and dedicated disabled changing and toilet areas.

© Rob Read

The kiosk and reception area have a utilitarian sixties or seventies feel about them, and it would be a sad day indeed if the period signage were ever to disappear. The typeface instantly evokes a time when the British public were spreading their wings and embracing progress after decades of war and austerity.

The most recent chapter in Pells's history is written in the paddling pool, recently refurbished and strikingly modern in feel compared to the main tank, which is large and filled with fresh, crisp unheated spring water.

There will be more history to be written at Pells, we are sure of it. The volunteer committee have already shown themselves to be inventive, an example of which was their hosting of the first writer in residence to be seen at a lido. In helping to showcase the mutually beneficial relationship between outdoor pools and creative arts, Pells has shown itself to be an historic pool with an eye on the future.

This is a super pool to visit by public transport, being a short walk from the station and bus routes. If you come by car you will need to park elsewhere in town and walk to the pool. This won't feel like a chore; Lewes itself shows a fine pair of ankles and there is much to admire as you travel its streets.

SALTDEAN LIDO

ENGLAND Sussex

Saltdean Lido

The Oval Park, Saltdean Park Road, Saltdean, Brighton

Sussex

BN2 8SP

- saltdeanlido-sales@fusion-lifestyle.com
- 01273 069984
- fusion-lifestyle.com/centres/saltdean
- @SaltdeanLido
- @SaltdeanLido
- @saltdeanlido

- 40 m x 18.5 m
- Corporately run on behalf of the council
- Seasonal
- Heated
- Freshwater
- Parking available on site
- Snack kiosk

It is a source of joy that Saltdean Lido has been saved from dereliction and disrepair by local enthusiasts determined to restore the fabulous outdoor pool, and its accompanying streamlined modern pavilion, for future generations.

Situated on the main coastal road east out of Brighton, at the village of Saltdean, this is the kind of pool you will spot from the road and just have to go and have a look. From the street you can look down into the hollow that shelters the lido from the wind coming off the sea and see the beauty of this pool and its buildings.

Built between 1937 and 1938, this unheated lido was huge. It has been named by English Heritage as one of the seven wonders of the English seaside, and rightly so, in our humble outdoor swimmers' opinion. Significant funds have been raised, including from the Heritage Lottery Fund, for the restoration and work started with the pool itself. In 2017 it reopened to the public, rebuilt

entirely and reduced in size. The original fountain was retained to lend that air of 1930s glamour that is so much a part of this place. When this book went to print work on the building had not commenced, and until that work is complete the changing facilities are basic, and temporary. Disabled swimmers are therefore not as well catered for as will be the case when the restoration is complete. Because this pool is a rapidly changing work in progress we recommend you call ahead to determine whether your particular needs can be met.

Even if you are not planning to swim at all the pools contained in this guide, we think that Saltdean is really worth adding to your bucket list. A visit here evokes a real sense of why lidos became so important in the UK – they brought sophistication to swimming in the open air that harnessed the experience of being on a Mediterranean beach. Saltdean made elements of a Riviera lifestyle accessible to all – particularly on a sunny south-coast day. A swim here was always a treat and now is again, with the promise of more to come as the pool is gradually restored.

ABBEY FIELDS OUTDOOR POOL

ENGLAND Warwickshire

Abbey Fields Outdoor Pool
Bridge Street, Kenilworth
Warwickshire
CV8 1BP

- abbeyfieldsinfo@everyoneactive.com
- 01926 855478
- everyoneactive.com/centre/abbey-fields-swimming-pool
- @eaAbbeyFields
- @eaAbbeyFields

- Irregular
- Corporately run on behalf of the council
- Seasonal
- Heated
- Freshwater
- Abbey Fields car park a short walk from site
- Snack kiosk

The Midlands is one of the areas of England that is the least populated with lidos. This seems, to us, faintly ridiculous when one considers how many people live in the area. That makes Abbey Fields rather special, and if you are doing an M40 lido road trip, and have already swum at Banbury and High Wycombe or are planning to swim there later in your trip, a starting or finishing swim in Warwickshire's only open-air swimming pool is a worthwhile option.

The outdoor pool is part of a bigger leisure centre. It is an irregularly shaped, modern heated pool that is plenty big enough for a swim or a leisurely dip and a potter around. The

whole site is a suntrap, so plan to spend some time basking after your swim.

Situated not far from Kenilworth Castle, Abbey Fields Leisure Centre has plenty of car parking for users, good changing facilities and lockers, and everything you would expect to find in a modern leisure centre – including comprehensive accessibility provision for disabled swimmers. This pool feels like a nice discovery, especially when fewer than 20 per cent of the UK's outdoor pools lie north of this one. At the time of going to print Warwickshire District Council had expressed intentions to replace the outdoor pool with an indoor training pool. There has been outdoor swimming on this site for over 100 years; to lose that would be a terrible blow to Kenilworth. Please call ahead and check the situation if you are planning to travel.

TISBURY SWIMMING POOL

ENGLAND Wiltshire

Tisbury Swimming Pool
Weaveland Road, Tisbury
Wiltshire
SP3 6HJ

- tisburyswimmingclub@gmail.com
- 01747 870896
- www.tisburyswimmingpool.co.uk
- @tisburypool
- Tisbury Swimming Pool

- 23 m x 9 m
- Volunteer run
- Seasonal
- Heated
- Freshwater
- Parking available on site
- Snack kiosk

© Helen De Meyer

Tisbury sits in the heart of Wiltshire, on the fringe of a pretty village solidly built from local stone. It's not likely to be high on your lido road trip hit list, if it's even on your radar at all. We encourage you to move it up a place or two.

The pool itself is of the no-frills variety, a useful-sized, well-maintained tank sitting in a comparatively small site. It operates a timetable of distinct sessions, so plan your visit carefully, and be aware that there is not always a lane in. If you have a solid workout in mind, you should definitely choose your session carefully; you're unlikely to achieve it if you turn up just after school lets out on a sunny day, for example. There

© Helen De Meyer

isn't a lot of kerb appeal, the buildings that are visible from the road being fairly plain, but you'll hear the happy sounds from within before you see the water. And it's the happiness of Tisbury that merits a lido road trip. You are likely to be greeted, if the pool is at all busy, with a joyous uproar that is the hallmark of children and families having a good time. It's evident that this is a community that loves its pool. If you enter into the spirit of that, channel your inner child, maybe treat yourself to an ice lolly after your swim, then you'll have a delightful time.

There is parking immediately outside, but some steps up to reception. There is, however, level access through a gate at the other side of the site and that can be opened on request. Currently there are no dedicated disabled toilet or changing facilities, but when this book went to print there were aspirations to install some, so calling ahead to check the situation would be worthwhile. Access into the water is by way of ladders only.

© Helen De Meyer

© Helen De Meyer

DROITWICH SPA LIDO

ENGLAND Worcestershire

HISTORIC POOLS OF BRITAIN

Droitwich Spa Lido
Lido Park, Worcester Road, Droitwich Spa
Worcestershire
WR9 8AA

- info@wychavonleisure.co.uk
- 01905 799342
- wychavonleisure.co.uk/our-centres/droitwich-spa-lido
- @RiversFitness
- @RiversDroitwich

- 40 m x 18 m
- Corporately run on behalf of
- Seasonal
- Heated
- Saltwater
- Pay and display car park on site
- On-site café

Droitwich is a brine town and, as you might expect, the lido makes good use of that. It is one of only two remaining brine-fed pools in the UK – the other being Nantwich.

Droitwich was built in the 1930s, and has always operated as a heated brine-fed pool. The pool was closed for a time in the early 2000s, but thanks to the efforts of the town it was not let go without a fight. That fight was ultimately successful, and a full refurbishment took place prior to reopening in 2007. The crisp, 1930s pavilion that marks the entrance remains preserved, but the tank itself has been completely modernised. At the far end of the pool is a beach-style sloping entry, complete with a fountain, and the rubber crumb surface is kind on the feet. A wheelchair can be made available to assist disabled swimmers into the water. A lane rope strung across the pool separates off the rest of the tank, sheltering the shallow water lovers from swimmers. This makes good use of the space, but it does mean that if you are swimming lengths there is only a wall at one end of each length. It's not a major inconvenience, but if you're a clock watcher you'll need to adjust your expectations about your times and turnarounds because you'll only get a push-off at one end.

The brine is, as is the case at Nantwich, diluted such that the salt is not overwhelming. On some days it's hard to detect any salt at all, and it can never be described as harsh in any way. The changing rooms are pleasingly modern, cater well for disabled swimmers and lie in the red-brick building that runs along one side of the pool. That also houses a café that is open to non-swimmers via access from the park side. There is plenty of space around the pool for spreading out towels on a warm day. Heated to 23°C, this pool might feel brisk on a warm day if you're more accustomed to the higher temperatures that seem to have become the norm at indoor leisure centres. But it is a temperature that is undoubtedly lovely once you're in, and on a cool day it'll feel like a warm bath.

ALPAMARE SCARBOROUGH WATERPARK

ENGLAND Yorkshire

Alpamare Scarborough Waterpark
North Bay, 28 Burniston Road, Scarborough
Yorkshire
YO12 6PH

- info@alpamare.co.uk
- 01723 81431
- alpamare.co.uk
- @AlpamareUK
- @AlpamareUK
- @AlpamareUK

- 200 sq m
- Privately run
- Year round
- Heated
- Freshwater
- Pay and display car park on site
- On-site café

There was a real debate about whether Alpamere was suitable to feature in this guide. It is a brand new indoor and outdoor swimming and leisure facility overlooking the North Sea at Scarborough on the north side of the town next to Scarborough Open Air Theatre. Its seaside location, concept and very attractive website pictures made it a definite yes to be included.

Why then do you detect notes of doubt that it should be included in *The Lido Guide*? There are a few reasons. This is a well-designed concept, with two outdoor pools heated to 28°C and a 35°C infinity pool that is a joy to be in even on the coldest days of the year. It is a smart leisure venue with complex indoor water slides, a wave-machine pool and other fun things for very little children through to teenagers and adults alike. The on-site café/restaurant serves proper meals as well as alcoholic, soft and hot drinks and ice cream. The changing rooms are lovely, well maintained, and cater well to the needs of disabled swimmers and overall the whole experience is one that has been well thought out.

The thing is, you can't really swim here. The two outdoor pools give you the best opportunity of doing this but the way the pools are both shaped underwater, with places to sit and lounge, means that you have to hog the middle of either of the 20-metre pools to be able to swim up and down. The other thing is that it is expensive. You are buying an experience that is cheaper to book and pay for online than in person on the day, and you commit to a four-hour ticket, which includes the time you spend getting changed at either end of your visit and any time you spend in the café – you can pay to stay longer than this but the timed session focuses the mind on how you spend your time while you are there.

It is great to see investment being put into new outdoor swimming facilities in the UK, and particularly in Yorkshire, where there used to be so many lidos (including one in Scarborough); there are now only three here. The 'however' hanging in the air is that it is an expensive visit *and* you pay for parking on top of the cost of entry. Ahem.

HELMSLEY OPEN AIR POOL

ENGLAND Yorkshire

Helmsley Open Air Pool
Baxton's Sprunt, Helmsley
Yorkshire
YO62 5HT

- info@helmsleyopenairpool.org
- 01439 408010
- helmsleyopenairpool.org
- @Helmsleylido
- @helmsleylido
- @helmsleyopenairpool

- 25 m x 8 m
- Volunteer run
- Seasonal
- Heated
- Freshwater
- Free parking available on site
- Snack kiosk

The open-air pool of Helmsley sits above this market town, next to the cricket pitch, a short walk from the centre of the action and the historic Helmsley castle. It is one of those towns that feels like it *should* have an open-air pool because of its North Yorkshire location, its popularity with locals and visitors alike and the historic warm stone feel of the whole place.

The pool itself is a standard 25 metres long and is heated. It is flanked by large areas to sit and enjoy a picnic or ice cream from the kiosk, and is ideal for swimming lengths or enjoying family fun with floats and the opportunity to dip in and out of the pool over an extended stay. Behind the doors of the plant room lies something unusual in UK pools – an air source heat exchanger. One can't help but think that it was a bold move to invest in such a thing, in a Yorkshire climate, given that they rely, unsurprisingly, on warm air. However, that vision paid off, because it has proved to be a cost-effective way to boost the temperature of the water.

Run by volunteers, this is one of those pools that has embedded itself in the community, with swimming lessons for locals, an artist in residence, annual fundraising events and an enthusiasm for getting kids active by way of a very popular aquathlon series. It is really worth a visit, and would make an ideal lido road trip with Stanhope/Weardale, Haltwistle and Ilkley pools.

When this book went to print European Union funding had been secured to make improvements to the site. We can't, therefore, comment reliably on what disabled access facilities might be available in future so please do call ahead to check.

ILKLEY LIDO

ENGLAND Yorkshire

Ilkley Lido
Denton Road, Ilkley
Yorkshire
LS29 0BZ

- None
- 01943 600453
- bradford.gov.uk/lido
- @SportBradford
- @BradfordSwimming

- 46 m diameter
- Council run
- Seasonal
- Unheated
- Freshwater
- Free parking available on site
- On-site café

One of only three (four if you include Alpamare) open-air pools in the UK's biggest county, Ilkley is a classic lido in a classic setting. This huge, unheated swimming pool with its iconic fountain has something for everyone. If the pool is huge, the grassy site it sits on, on the north side of the River Wharfe, is probably the biggest we've seen for any lido in the country.

Situated on the opposite bank to the centre of Ilkley, but still within walking distance of the railway station and with an equally big car park, this is a very accessible, well signposted and easy-to-use open-air pool.

The lido has a non-standard shape but has, at its centre, a rectangular area perfect for swimming lengths flanked by semicircular areas for relaxing swims or water play. The whole area is surrounded by lawned areas to sit on and while away the day as you enjoy its spectacular setting in the Yorkshire Dales.

There is a café on site at the top of the steps overlooking the lido serving snacks, ice creams and sweets and enabling you to stay all day. The whole complex also houses a standard indoor pool that is accessible year round and helps to make the site a sustainable and valuable resource. Although it is run by Bradford Council, the Friends of Ilkley Lido are a huge voluntary force for good in making this such a fantastic open-air pool.

Most notably they work actively to keep the opening hours as broad as possible and generate a huge crowd for their summer solstice swim – a treat in the outdoor swimming calendar if ever there was one. In the past there has been winter swimming at Ilkley Lido, but at the time of going to print that seemed to be in something of a state of flux, so contact the lido directly to enquire about this if it interests you.

This is such an iconic swimming pool, many miles north of concentrated lido country, and so worth a visit if you are anywhere near. A lido road trip taking in Ilkley, Helmsley and Ingleton would be one big Yorkshire swimming treat.

As you'd expect with a facility of this age, it hasn't been designed with modern accessibility standards in mind. However, a lot of effort has clearly gone into making this facility as accessible as possible, and we would really like to commend Bradford council for the online information they provide, in partnership with disabledgo.com. It is easily the most comprehensive we've seen on a lido website, and allows disabled swimmers to have a detailed understanding of the place before arriving.

INGLETON SWIMMING POOL

ENGLAND Yorkshire

Ingleton Swimming Pool
Sammy Lane, Ingleton
Yorkshire
LA6 3EG

- ingletonpool@gmail.com
- 01524 241147
- ingletonpool.co.uk
- @IngletonPool
- Ingleton Outdoor Swimming Pool

- 20 m x 8 m
- Volunteer run
- Seasonal
- Heated
- Freshwater
- Parking available in the village
- Snack kiosk

To reach Ingleton Swimming Pool you need to leave your car in the centre of the village and follow the signs that take you to the path to the pool. This generates the feeling that the pool is part of some secret wooded grotto, and it isn't far away from that in reality. Ingleton is quite a steep village and the pool is situated at the bottom of the valley near the river. Glimpses of it come into view before you reach the steps down to the pool. Friendly volunteers will greet you at the door, and they also run the kiosk, selling snacks and drinks.

This is a 20-metre heated pool, accessed via ladders only, which has a simply glorious setting in a shady glade and it is a popular spot with locals and visitors alike. One side of the pool terrace offers seating, with tables and chairs at the highest level that enjoy a view over the whole pool.

There has been investment in this pool in recent years as the result of the work of volunteers, who not only keep the pool open each year but raise money to keep the lights and heating on and improve the pool environment. The separate male and female communal changing rooms are of a decent size and located right on the poolside. That makes it as easy as possible to get changed quickly and get in the pool for some laps, or the ever-popular repeated jumping in from the deep end! There are dedicated disabled shower/toilet and changing facilities.

There are cafés and places to eat in Ingleton after your swim and parking is plentiful in the village, mainly in pay and display car parks (this is a busy tourist area in the Yorkshire Dales). Swimmers with reduced mobility will find the ramped access to the pool helpful, although there is at least a 200-metre walk from the nearest parking. This pool would make a lovely addition to either a Cumbrian lido road trip, or on a coast-to-coast trip taking in a swim at Yorkshire's other lovely pools en route to Helmsley.

Nearby there is plenty to see and do, including a visit to Ingleton Falls or a trip to see the Ribblehead Viaduct on the Settle to Carlisle Railway.

The Rock Pool, County Down

NORTHERN IRELAND

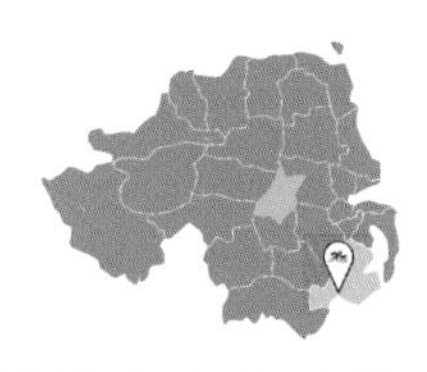

THE ROCK POOL

NORTHERN IRELAND County Down

The Rock Pool
South Promenade, Newcastle
County Down
BT33 0AA

- info@therockpool.co.uk
- 02843 725034
- therockpool.co.uk
- @RockPoolNewcastle

- Large
- Council run
- Seasonal
- Unheated
- Saltwater
- Free parking available in adjacent car park
- None available

The Rock Pool is one of those open-air pools that has the capacity to take the seasoned and traditional lido lover's breath away (and not just from jumping into the unheated seawater that fills the pool!). Entry to the pool is from the coastal road approximately 1 mile south of Newcastle and it has the kind of beguiling entrance that belies the view once you step through the turnstile.

The square, turquoise-walled pool that stretches out beneath you and into the sea shouts, 'Get in quickly!' and the yellow-doored individual changing rooms at street level are an inviting sunny sight, particularly on what might be a grey day for swimming.

You can catch glimpses of the pool from the adjacent sizeable car park, creating that sense of anticipation of an outdoor swim

we've referred to elsewhere in the book. The mix of the blues of the pool, the yellow of the changing-room doors and the red of the pool lettering really work here to evoke a sense of holidays past, and it's a lovely place to stay all day, dipping in and out of the water

We won't pretend that this is the easiest pool to find. Geographically, it is very straight-forward once you know about it, but information about the pool and its opening times weren't that easy to locate when we first started looking. Somehow it is worth it, though. This pool feels like the essence of what this guide is all about – finding a gem of a swimming pool you might not otherwise have known about.

The changing levels on this site might present some challenges to swimmers with reduced mobility. Once poolside it is reasonably flat, and as well as ladders there are concrete steps into the water – although the handrail does not extend the length of the steps.

TROPICANA WARM SEA POOLS

NORTHERN IRELAND County Down

Tropicana Warm Sea Pools
Central Promenade, Newcastle
County Down
BT33 0AA

- nlc.reception@nmandd.org
- 02843 725034
- downdc.gov.uk/Leisure---Culture/Leisure-Centres/Newcastle.aspx
- @nmdcouncil
- @nmdcouncil

- Irregular
- Council run
- Seasonal
- Heated
- Freshwater
- On-street pay and display parking in Newcastle
- None available

We've only found two open-air swimming pools in Northern Ireland; that they are less than a mile away from each other and both operated by the same local council in the seaside town of Newcastle on the Antrim coast is a source of both joy, that they exist here, and puzzlement that other seaside towns in Northern Ireland haven't managed to retain their pools.

They are two very, very different pools. However, between them they provide something for everyone. Tropicana is a heated seawater pool in the centre of Newcastle, next to the leisure centre and across the road from a host of shops, cafés and amusements with local pay and display parking. Inside the pool there are plenty of things to keep families amused for a number of hours and the heated water prevents little ones in particular from getting cold as they enjoy this pool and its slides and amusements.

This is an irregularly shaped pool that is less than a metre deep in most places. So, can you swim in it? Yes, you can. But you have to come with an open mind, probably with children, and recognise that this isn't intended as a lap pool. It is big enough to swim and play in, and the pool is surrounded by places to sit. It is fun place to be in the water outside on the promenade.

The changing rooms on the side of the pool are communal, and there are refreshments available in the pool complex as well as locally.

Gourock Pool, Renfrewshire

SCOTLAND

STONEHAVEN OPEN AIR SWIMMING POOL

SCOTLAND Aberdeenshire

Stonehaven Open Air Swimming Pool
Queen Elizabeth Park, Stonehaven
Aberdeenshire
AB39 2RD

- friends@stonehavenopenairpool.co.uk,
- 01569 762134 (01569 763162 pre-season)
- stonehavenopenairpool.co.uk
- @StoneyPool
- @StonehavenHeatedOpenAirPool

- 50 m x 20 m
- Council run, in cooperation with volunteers
- Seasonal
- Heated
- Saltwater
- Free parking available on site
- On-site café

Those experiences that fall at the outer extremes of the bell curve are often the most memorable. By definition they aren't the norm; they have a rare power over us that does not come with the humdrum of the everyday. Stonehaven, the UK's most northerly lido, holds such power. Its geography, on the shore of the North Sea at a more northerly latitude than Moscow, places it beyond the average, as does the heated seawater that fills it. The bright colours of the buildings and terraces that surround the pool have a power to lift the spirits on a grey, northerly day that borders on magical. In the sunshine it is a feast for the visual senses, a riot of primary colours and crisp shadows.

Swimmers can expect this pool to deliver warmth beyond its water. There is a relaxed and cooperative approach to activities that some pools are

naturally inclined to be stuffy about, such as photography and flinging yourself down the slide head-first. Swimmers are trusted to manage themselves and get along nicely with each other without a forest of signage and the endless shrill of the lifeguard's whistle.

The changing rooms are pleasingly vintage without being tired, and there is a wealth of unobtrusive period detail for

lovers of 1930s architecture. This isn't the grandest example of that period, but it is no less fascinating for that and there is a great deal of pleasure to be had from noticing the small things. The pool was built to competition standards of the day, so it's large enough to feel like a rare treat in today's 25-metre world. There is a hoist, and the site is wheelchair accessible. Carers are also admitted free of charge.

The café that sits alongside the pool is well worth drying and dressing to sit inside a while if, like us, you are fascinated by the history of a pool. There is a wealth of material on display on the walls. Swimmers who don't want the trouble of drying off are served via a takeaway window. There can be few simple pleasures as captivating as eating cheesy chips on the terraces in the sunshine, still clad in slightly damp and salty togs. Take plenty of pennies, however, as at the time of writing the café was cash only.

This pool is also remarkable for its operating model. It is a very successful example of a community organisation working hand in hand with a local authority to secure the future of a much-loved asset. The local authority operates the pool, and the Friends of Stonehaven Open Air Swimming Pool devote many volunteer hours to maintaining, promoting and enhancing the pool, and to the fundraising required to support that activity. That spirit of cooperation is a thing to be cherished and admired.

TAMAR MANOUKIAN NEW CUMNOCK POOL

SCOTLAND Ayrshire

Tamar Manoukian New Cumnock Pool
Castle Street, New Cumnock
Ayrshire
KA18 4AH

info@dumfries-house.org.uk
01290 333891
dumfries-house.org.uk/attractions/new-cumnock-pool
@NewCumnockPool
@NCSPool
@newcumnockpool

25 m x 10 m
Charitable trust run
Seasonal
Heated
Freshwater
Free parking available on site
None available

Pledger pic: *Evan, Michael and Gareth Williams*

New Cumnock is a town that many may be unfamiliar with, even within Scotland. It is a small, fairly rural community, set in softly rolling countryside. It seems an unlikely place for a gleaming beauty of a pool such as this. Until one remembers that before outdoor pools became comparatively scarce, many small communities had their own. This pool was built in the mid-1960s, and the fact that it gleams today is thanks to an extensive refurbishment, by the Dumfries House Trust, in 2017.

The pool now offers what feels like a contemporary, smart hotel-pool-experience. The pool surrounds and tank are tiled in a uniform finish, giving a seamlessly sleek look. The surrounds can be a little slippery in the rain, however, so consider taking flip-flops or similar. This is a pool that you shouldn't be put off visiting by rain. The water is heated into the high twenties Celsius, the indoor changing rooms offer all the warmth and comforts one would expect of a modern facility, and cater well for disabled swimmers, while the poolside changing cubicles will keep those who prefer a bit of fresh air under their

towels happy. Those cubicles, with doors painted in shades to perfectly accentuate the view of the hills beyond, and the green-roofed clock house-style entrance, lend an old-fashioned lido feel to what is now, in every other sense, a thoroughly modern facility.

We highly recommend a sunset swim when the sun punches through the glass bricks in the wall at the shallow end, throwing patterns on the water, and the low-slung light bounces off the hills in the distance beyond the deep end.

There is no on-site catering, and not a great deal on offer close by, so lido road trippers (or train trippers – there is a station about fifteen minutes' walk from the pool) may wish to bring a picnic.

THE TRINKIE AND NORTH BATHS

SCOTLAND Caithness

The Trinkie and North Baths
Wick Bay
Caithness
KW1 5TN

- None
- None
- None
- @wickheritage
- @friendsofthetrinkie and @WickHeritageMuseum

- Approximately 30 m x 10 m
- Volunteer run
- Seasonal
- Unheated
- Saltwater
- Free parking on the coast road adjacent to the path to the pool
- None available

The Trinkie is the UK's most northerly sea pool, and North Baths lies close by. You'll find Trinkie around three-quarters of a mile south of the town of Wick and accessed via a beach path from the coastal road, where parking is free. We've truly debated whether or not these are lidos, and whether they should be included in *The Lido Guide*, but we've erred on the side of saying yes to these pools because there is just about enough space to get a decent swim in and there is a man-made element to both. There is no lifeguard, but swimming here is free, and the pools are definitely publicly accessible.

The water is very cold, and the pool is filled by the high tide, which then reveals the pool at low tide – there is a group of volunteers, Friends of the Trinkie, who have, in the past, spent time cleaning and painting the inside of the Trinkie white prior to the summer season. The local heritage museum, run by the Wick Society, is the keeper of the history of the pools, and we have provided their contact details as they're well worth a visit. They are also worth calling if you are planning to swim in either of these pools – whether you are travelling specifically for a swim here or are planning to be in the area anyway. Each pool was visited in 2018 and although they both looked like they needed considerable work they also looked like they could possibly be swimmable. Please check before you head to Wick to swim there.

At these pools you can expect a dinky, fairly wild experience with no airs and graces and nothing to ease access for disabled swimmers.

TRINKIE

PITTENWEEM TIDAL POOL

SCOTLAND Fife

Pittenweem Tidal Pool
West Braes, Pittenweem
Fife
KY10 2PT is close by

- None
- None
- Opening times for the West Braes toilets near the poolfifecoastalpath.co.uk/downloads/2018-toilet-opening-times/pittenweem-west-braes.aspx
- @TheWestBraes
- @TheWestBraes
- @thewestbraesproject

- Approximately 50 m x 20 m
- Volunteer run
- Seasonal
- Unheated
- Saltwater
- Parking available at West Braes car park next to the crazy golf and (seasonal) toilets
- None available

Pittenweem Tidal Pool is one of those evocative places where you can almost hear the shrieks and laughs from the lido in its previous incarnation as a summer hotspot. This large, walled tidal pool is at the bottom of concrete steps down from the playground and crazy golf course in the active fishing village of Pittenweem in the East Neuk of Fife.

There used to be a large clifftop pavilion, changing rooms, a pontoon and crowds at this lido, but nowadays there is just a small sandy beach that leads down to the pool. It has a sloping entry and a rocky bottom as you gradually enter the clear but cold water, step by step. We estimate this pool is probably about 50 metres by 20 metres in total, but it isn't a long-course swim, as you can only really start swimming about halfway in and you'll need flip-flops or sand

shoes if you want to get over the stones without sore feet!

It is a lovely swim, however. The spot is sheltered, the water has a gentle feel to it and it holds the memory of yesteryear – the concrete wall at the end of the pool still shows the signs of where the handrail used to be and the steps at this depth are still clearly there, although very weathered. Go at low tide on a lovely evening and this might seem like your own private piece of heaven just off the coastal path.

Some wriggling under a towel will be needed to get changed at either end of the swim, as there are no changing facilities on the beach and only seasonally open toilets on the clifftop. In the daytime there are a couple of cafés in town for a post-swim cuppa, and there is the option of fish and chips from the Larachmhor Tavern on the harbourside if you are there in the evening. This is a small and seasonal place, although the hardy could swim in the pool year round; this pool is worth a visit if you are in the area and the tide is out. You can do a coast-to-coast lido road trip if you want to swim in Gourock during the day, too, or if you are heading up or down the east coast of Scotland, Stonehaven is a possibility.

Swimmers with a disability affecting mobility are likely to find this pool extremely challenging to access in its current virtually wild state. A community group, the West Braes Project, are working to maintain and improve the pool, but it is not likely accessibility will be improved in the short term.

INVERNESS LEISURE CENTRE

SCOTLAND Inverness-shire

Inverness Leisure Community Multi-use Sports Centre
Bught Park, Inverness
Caithness
IV3 5SS

- info@invernessleisure.co.uk
- 01463 667500
- highlandlife.com/il/s
- @hlhsport
- @invernessleisure

- 5 m diameter max
- Council run
- Seasonal
- Heated
- Freshwater
- Free parking available on site
- On-site café

This isn't really a lido. We've included it because it fits our definition of a publicly accessible outdoor pool with man-made sides and because it is a very small outdoor pool in the very north of Scotland and is curiously in the shape of a thistle. There are no laps to be done here. It forms the end point of a lazy river in the leisure pool of the local sports centre. But when you are an enthusiast, it is difficult not to want to mention every patch of publicly accessible open-air water you know about, and if you are in the area, you might want to go to this indoor pool for a swim in the knowledge that there is a tiny bit of outdoor-water activity designed into the pool.

We don't have an image of Inverness Leisure Centre, so here are some other Scottish pools to whet your appetite.

Above: *Gourock Pool, Renfrewshire*

Above: *Stonehaven Open Air Swimming Pool, Aberdeenshire*

GOUROCK POOL

SCOTLAND Renfrewshire

Gourock Pool
Albert Road, Gourock
Renfrewshire

lauren.o'donnell@inverclydeleisure.com
01475 213122
inverclydeleisure.com/enterprise/GourockPool
@InverclydeL
@InverclydeLeisure

33 m x 17 m
Corporately run on behalf of the council
Seasonal
Heated
Saltwater
Free parking available on site
Snack kiosk

Gourock clings to the shores of the Clyde like a limpet. On a wild, steel-grey day it is a beacon of blue; the heated seawater feels like sanctuary.

The architecture of the place is reminiscent of an ocean liner. As you enter at street level there is a spacious sundeck from which to view the pool and the spectacular hills that lie across the water. The ironwork of the handrails adds further to the air of luxury ocean-going travel, and descending the stairs to the pool deck invokes a feeling of anticipation (there is a lift available for swimmers who might find the stairs difficult); the salt tang sharpens in the nostrils, the soft splash of swimmers mingles with the sounds of the sea and as the view across the water recedes behind the sea wall, one feels cocooned.

The changing rooms are at pool-deck level, and thanks to recent refurbishment that saw almost £2 million invested, they are modern, sleek and well equipped for disabled swimmers. When the Scottish weather does its worst they offer welcome shelter to swimmers, but in the best weather it is easy to imagine they might be redundant as swimmers spread their towels out on the ample paved surrounds around the toddler pool, and linger to enjoy the riot of blue. This is definitely a pool that shines in poor weather, however. The contrast of the blue and white against the rolling grey of a heavy sky is a sight that swimmers can feel lucky to enjoy if they take the time to float on their backs and drink it in.

Gourock retains diving boards, which open subject to capacity and weather. Atop the boards a tantalising glimpse of the views beyond can be had before one launches into the water. Diving boards still in use are becoming a rarity in outdoor pools, and the fact that these remain after the refurbishment of the pool lifts the heart. There are good, gently sloping steps down into the shallow end, and a hoist is also available.

Catering on site is limited to vending machines, but as the high street is a few steps away this isn't too great a problem. Swimmers will need to be aware that the car park next to the pool uses a card display system, and the parking cards can be obtained from local shops. The system is a very effective way of offering free, time-limited parking. When we visited we had plenty of time within the free window of parking for a leisurely swim and an even more leisurely lunch in a local café.

Lido Ponty, Rhondda Cynon Taf

WALES

LIDO PONTY

WALES Rhondda Cynon Taf

Lido Ponty
Ynysangharad War Memorial Park, Pontypridd
Rhondda Cynon Taf
CF37 4PE

- lidoponty@rctcbc.gov.uk
- 03000 040000
- lidoponty.co.uk
- @LidoPonty
- @LidoPonty
- @lidoponty

- 25 m
- Council owned
- Seasonal
- Heated
- Freshwater
- Four car parks within walking distance at Gas Road (CF37 2AA), Goods Yard (CF37 5RG), Sardis Road (CF37 1LE) and Ty Pennant (CF37 2FW)
- On-site café

It is a source of much sadness to us that Wales has only one lido. It used to be peppered with outdoor pools, many in the south of the country having been built by miners' benevolent societies for the benefit of local residents at a time when indoor sanitation was a rarity. They were fine examples of often impoverished communities pulling together to make a difference to everyone. One by one those pools have fallen into disrepair and closed, often as a result of local authority cuts, and there are few realistic campaigns to resurrect them. Brynaman is the most likely to succeed, but even that will take a great deal of time and a herculean effort.

Lido Ponty is the result of just such an effort. There has been a lido in Ynysangharad Park for many years, and it fell derelict a few years ago, a dangerous eyesore blighting the park in a town that lies in one of the most economically disadvantaged parts of the UK. Resurrection seemed a hopeless cause – until significant Heritage Lottery and European Union funding was secured and a rebirth was finally possible.

The result is a spankingly modern facility that wouldn't be out of place in a Mediterranean holiday resort, but which also retains bags of period features and charm. The heritage of this place is written all over it, from the fascias to the changing cubicles and all points in between. The restoration made use of traditional skills, and ongoing maintenance continues to do that wherever possible. The once vast and solitary tank has been rebuilt to consist of three separate tanks, the heritage of the original retained in the shape of the white line that surrounds them. There is a tank for lane swimmers, another for dippers and splashers featuring a shallow beach-style area, and finally one for other activities such as pedal boats.

The traditional poolside changing is complemented with modern, heated, indoor changing rooms and you can choose to shower either indoors or outdoors. The outdoor showers are a real treat, as they offer a superb view of the hills surrounding the town. There is a newly built café and function room, and the former benefits from a kiosk that serves food poolside. The café has little in the way of individual charm, but it isn't unpleasant.

It is necessary to plan your visit here carefully if coming any distance, but you really should travel here to see what the future of lidos could look like if only the investment was more widely made. The local authority kept the pool free to use for the first two seasons, and at time of writing a small charge of just £1 per adult had been introduced. That low charge is testament to the wider economic benefits that the high number of visitors has brought to the area. The high footfall is why you need to plan carefully. Tickets are sold online for prebookable one-hour slots. There are a small number of tickets available on the door but if you haven't prebooked it is very likely you won't be able to swim if the weather is decent.

You also need to be aware that there is no parking at all on site, although you can drive down to drop off passengers with reduced mobility before going to park. If you are a disabled driver you should telephone in advance to see what arrangements can be made, as the nearest car parks are a fifteen-minute walk away, as is the train station. Once inside, the disabled access provision is excellent.

CHANNEL ISLANDS

La Valette Bathing Pools, Guernsey

LA VALLETTE BATHING POOLS

CHANNEL ISLANDS Guernsey

HISTORIC POOLS OF BRITAIN

La Vallette Bathing Pools
Saint Peter Port
Guernsey
GY1 4NF

- LaValletteChallenge@gmail.com
- None
- None
- @BathingPools
- @lavalletteproject

- Three pools, different sizes – two approximately 20 m x 15 m and one approximately 50 m x 20 m
- Council run in partnership with volunteers
- Year round
- Unheated
- Saltwater
- Disc/meter parking available on road nearby
- Snack kiosk

This is not a swimming destination on a lido road trip as you need to be in the area for other reasons (or committed to a lido air trip or lido ferry trip!) to swim at La Vallette. Is it worth it? If you are a lido enthusiast who enjoys a cold-water experience, or you are interested to see the work of hundreds of volunteers who have restored these historic swimming pools, then definitely add this to your list of would-like-to swims.

From the airport a bus takes you into Saint Peter Port – the journey is good value, scenic, and rather quaintly the bus stops at both recognised stops and for those putting their hand out

from the roadside. Once in the centre of Saint Peter Port, with its blue postboxes and yellow phone boxes, it is around a 1-kilometre walk along the promenade to the pools on the south side of the town.

There are three pools and a horseshoe bathing area at La Vallette, and while they are all close together they are distinct and separate pools – best to know this if you want to swim in all of them, as it does require you to walk along the roadside between them and not everyone fancies doing this clad only in swimwear.

The first pool you come to was the last one to be restored – the gentleman's pool. Previously only for men and involving a fee to swim, the pool is now both free and for mixed bathing. There is a really good opportunity for a decent swim in this rhombus-shaped swimming pool, as well as the feel of an infinity pool looking out towards Castle Cornet when the tide fills it twice a day. Further along the road you come to the almost 50-metre length ladies' and smaller children's pools and the toilets and café atop the changing block. All three glorious pools are refreshed by the sea and have the kind of weathered look that only sea pools can really achieve – the diving platform on the main pool allowing you access into deep, refreshing saltwater looks both robust and a testament to taking on the wind and rain of many storms. These pools were all badly damaged during the storms of February 2014, and volunteers have worked to raise money to restore them. All seem well used by locals, with school swimming lessons happening in the shallow end of the children's pool, and lunchtime lap swimmers and triathletes making good use of the ladies' pool and quick-dip users of the gentleman's pool.

All the pools are free to use. The kiosk has a hot and cold menu and is well priced, and the free toilets near the children's pool are big enough to get changed in. Although there is a changing block underneath the café, you need to be there at the same time a good-natured local member with a key is arriving or leaving to use the changing and shower facilities. There are no facilities other than an open-sided shelter at the gentleman's pool, so some wriggling under a towel here is probably required to change before and after your swim.

A swim here would make a good lido trip with a swim at Havre Des Pas Lido in Saint Helier in Jersey.

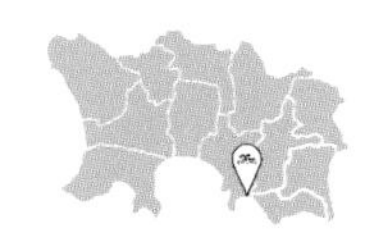

HAVRE DES PAS BATHING POOL

CHANNEL ISLANDS Jersey

Havre Des Pas Bathing Pool
Havre Des Pas
Jersey
JE2 4UL

- eversholtswimmingpool@gmail.com
- 01525 280515
- gov.je/leisure/sport/activecard/facilities/outdoor/pages/havredespas.aspx
- @lidojersey

- At least 150 m wide (approximate and estimated)
- Council run
- Seasonal
- Heated
- Saltwater
- Parking available on in nearby pay and display car parks
- On-site café

Like La Vallette on Guernsey, there are two large sea pools/marine lakes in Saint Helier, Jersey that you can only get to from mainland UK by plane or ferry. The best-known one is at Havre Des Pas, a purpose-built lido area on the beach that is filled by the tide, allowing for significant long-course swimming, hanging out or taking a breather on the pontoon mid-pool or pootling about enjoying being immersed in cool seawater in the open air. There is room here for it all.

Situated on the south-east side of the island and approximately 1.5 kilometres from both the ferry terminal and centre of town, this is the archetype of a lido. The boardwalk access, blue, white and yellow colourways, changing block with toilets, poolside shower, kiosk selling ice creams and attentive lifeguards on duty between 10 a.m.–6 p.m.

in the summer season all make this an ideal place to idle away several hours.

The slope down to the beach from the promenade makes this among the most accessible sea pools we've found, and although the cobbles may prove tricky for initial access, once on the beach the graduated entry into the pool

makes a swim here possible for those able or wanting to wade or paddle their way into the water rather than accessing it down submerged steps further along the lido walls.

Although there is limited parking nearby on the street or in small car parks and there is no parking specifically for the lido, this is a well-organised, well-managed set-up for an outdoor pool, with the capacity for many people to swim and relax at the same time.

The other outdoor pool in Saint Helier is the Victoria Marine Lake, in view of the Elizabeth Castle nearer to the centre of town on the north-west side of the harbour. Originally built to mark the diamond jubilee of Queen Victoria, it was restored in 2014, and at 190 metres by 150 metres provides a significant sheltered sea-filled swimming space on the promenade at West Park. It doesn't have the same resources as the Havre Des Pas Lido as there are no lifeguards, changing rooms or other facilities here, but it does offer the same long-range outdoor swimming experience and sparkles on a warm day when the tide is out. To find one amazing large lido here is a joy; to find two is slightly overwhelming, but makes it potentially worth the visit to Jersey for the swimming alone.

A swim here would also make a good lido trip combined with La Vallette, Guernsey.

OOL DEPTH 1.2m

YOU SAY LEE-DOH, WE SAY LY-DOH

We have separated two open-air pools out as belonging to the lido community but being rather different from the other entries in this book. Bristol Lido and the Thames Lido in Reading (formerly known as King's Meadow) are both restored Victorian open-air pools with restaurants and spas alongside. In both cases painstaking work has brought the pools back to life. We've included them in this guide because while their primary business is the restaurant trade, they very definitely remain lidos, but note that public access to them is significantly more expensive than other pools in the book. Casual swimming is possible at restricted times; at other times the pool is only available to members, or those using the spa.

We say ly-doh. They say lee-doh.

BRISTOL LIDO

ENGLAND Bristol

Bristol Lido
Oakfield Place, Clifton
Bristol
BS8 2BJ

- spa@lidobristol.com
- 01179 339530
- lidobristol.com
- @lidobristol
- @lidospaandrestaurant
- @lidobristol

- 24 m x 10 m
- Privately run
- Year round
- Heated
- Freshwater
- Pay and display parking at Clifton Down Shopping Centre (BS8 2NN) or West End car park (BS8 1EH)
- On-site restaurant

We've said several times in this guide that some open-air swimming pools are not that easy to find, and even when you get there you wonder if you are in the right place. And so it is with Bristol Lido. It is not a case of blink and you'll miss it, but one of those 'can it really be down here?' places, as this open-air pool is set in a series of narrow streets and Georgian terraces to the north of the city centre of Bristol.

From the outside there are few clues to what lies beyond – there is an entrance into the poolside restaurant that is open from breakfast through to dinner, and a specific portico entrance to the pool on the narrower side of the building. Stepping inside, you wonder how they could have fitted so much onto such a small footprint – that applies equally to the developers and owners of the current incarnation of the lido, and to their Victorian forefathers

who built it in the first place.

In format, the lido is very similar to its more recent sibling Thames Lido in Reading – large, square, blue tiles line the gently heated, constant-depth pool, and changing cubicles with their own shower edge one side of the deck with the plate-glass windows and onlookers of the bar lining the other. Like its sister pool, this is a great example of how an historic pool can have new life pumped into it with vision, determination, multiple income streams and a significant restoration budget.

THAMES LIDO

ENGLAND Berkshire

Thames Lido
Napier Road, Reading
Berkshire
RG1 8FR

- events@thameslido.com
- 01182 070640
- thameslido.com
- @ThamesLido
- @thameslido
- @thameslido

- 25 m x 8 m
- Privately run
- Year round
- Heated
- Freshwater
- Small private car park reserved for pre-booked spa packages or public King's Meadow NCP car park on Napier Road (RG1 8DF)
- On-site restaurant

History passes us by so easily. Any of you using the mainline rail service from Wales and the west of England to London Paddington will have passed through Reading. If you troubled yourselves to look out of the window at Reading station, away from the glass and stone-clad monolith office blocks, you might have noticed a low-slung, vaguely quaint, red brick building with steeply pitched tiled roofs. You could, however, be freely forgiven for having overlooked it. It isn't grand; in the past, it wasn't particularly tidy and it wasn't inviting.

But behind those walls lies history. This was King's Meadow Pool. Near derelict and overlooked for a long time, it has been revived as Thames Lido; history has become the future. This pool, like its sister in Bristol, is barely publicly accessible. There are limited

opening hours for a public swim. There are swim and dine, and spa day packages available that make the experience better value for money, but it will still require some outlay. That's the bad news.

So, what's the good news? Almost everything else. The team behind these pools are smart, creative, hip and commercially savvy. Thames Lido is a luxurious bolt-hole of year-round heated glory. The architecture is slickly modern, but retains important links to the past. The pool is plenty big enough for a decent swim, but we urge you to break from that a while to enjoy the surroundings. There are nods to lido heritage in the cedar poolside changing barrels and striped curtains, and the original woodwork frames the double-height glazing while trees whisper over the ridge tiles. This is the sort of pool that feels, from the luxurious spa products in the individual changing cubicles to the infinity-style raised deck-level tank, like a treat. Even if you are lucky enough to swim here regularly it would still, we imagine, feel like a treat. Every single day. Not least if you eat in the restaurant afterwards – the food is distinctive and delicious.

For that reason, you should save your pennies and put Thames Lido on your lido road trip wish list.

Parking at this pool is scarce, and limited to pre-booked day-package customers only. So you could get your chauffeur to drop you off, or you could take the train; Reading station is an easy ten-minute walk from the pool.

BACK IN THE SWIM OF THINGS

It is always the case that the minute something goes to print it is already out of date, and this is especially true of lidos.

Each year we hear about those open-air pools that can no longer be sustained in their community, or whose administrative bodies have succumbed to political pressure to do something else with the resources or the land the pool sits on.

Joyously, each year also brings the news that new groups, almost always formed of volunteers, have risen to resurrect, fundraise and lobby for the reopening of open-air pools from the past. There have been recent success stories like Broomhill in Ipswich and Saltdean Lido in Sussex – both featured in this guide in a way that wouldn't have been possible just a few short years ago. There remains strong work in progress to save or resurrect Grange-over-Sands Lido, Cleveland Pools in Bath, Otley Lido in Yorkshire, Tarlair in Scotland, and Brynaman and Abergavenny in Wales. Sometimes there are even opportunities for brand new pools, like the Thames Baths, which will rise and fall with the tidal river near Blackfriars in London, Sea Lanes in Brighton, where a seafront 50-metre lido is being planned, and in Ivybridge, where a pool with a sliding roof is under development. And as this book went to press Albert Road in Hull looked set to be restored for public swimming.

We have tried to include all the open-air pools that we know about in this guide, but it is possible that the occasional one or two have slipped through the net. Some haven't made it because they are not publicly accessible even though we know that they exist. If you know of one we haven't found, please tell us via social media; we hope there'll be a next edition of this guide updated to include any we've missed alongside any newly opened or reopened lidos.

We're going to end the guide with photographs of a very special place, Kimpton Pool Club. This 23-metre lido is the last family-owned lido in the country, and sits in the back garden of the owners' home. It has been welcoming swimmers from the wider community for over eighty years on a membership-only basis. The membership basis means that this pool is not publicly accessible, and it does not, therefore, meet the criteria for inclusion in this guide. But it is beautiful, and unique, and we celebrate that.

Kimpton Pool Club, Hertfordshire

Above: *Gourock Pool, Renfrewshire* © Souter & Stanley

ACKNOWLEDGEMENTS

For us, one of the most humbling aspects of this project has been the overwhelming tide of help, support and advice that has been generously given along the way.

Some special thanks are owed by us.

We'd like, most of all, to thank our pledgers. Their patronage is the single biggest reason you are holding this book in your hands. They didn't just believe in this book, they were willing to invest in that belief, and in us. We will forever be grateful to them.

Jenny Landreth, author of *Swimming London* and *Swell: A Waterbiography*, has been swimming in, thinking about and writing about lidos for even longer than we have. She has given us moral support, practical advice and acted as a sounding board for all our trials, tribulations and triumphs. She is wise, patient, sharp, effortlessly cool and side-splittingly funny. Thank you, Jenny.

Gideon Bright, founder of the UK-based success story that is Dryrobe, got in touch to explore ways he and his company could help with the project. From that was born the Dryrobe pledge level, and we are grateful for that very practical support at an early stage. Dryrobes are quite rightly loved by swimmers, and you'll see them crop up in images in the book. In winter, particularly, an unheated lido is their natural territory.

Many of the lidos featured in the book have been hugely enthusiastic about this book, and some staff and volunteers have been particularly supportive. Particular thanks are due to Angie Butler of Jubilee Sea Pool, Pam Barrett of Buckfastleigh, Rob Read of Pells Pool (not least for his sterling work maintaining a list of all UK lidos to have a social media presence), Andy and Barbara Thatcher of Portishead Open Air Pool and Joe Stanhope of Jubilee Park.

Other swimmers have provided an endless source of conversation and understanding about their favourite outdoor pools, lido road trips and quests they've undertaken. Sarah Thelwall was generous with her experiences, insights and photographs from over a hundred pools she's swum in and Helen De Meyer has also shared many a tale of similar numbers of lido visits across the UK by public transport, as well as allowing us to use some of her photographs in the book. Thank you both.

Finally, we'd like to acknowledge three of the many artists who are inspired by lidos and who, in turn, inspire us.

Stu Watkins from Oshe Design, and Liese Souter & Sarah Stanley – we salute you. Thanks for your enthusiasm for this book, and for the support you offer to pools.

Oshe Design – www.oshedesign.com

Souter & Stanley – www.souterandstanley.co.uk

Above: *Tooting Bec Lido, London* © Oshe Design

LANE OF FAME PLEDGERS

Andrew Caldwell

John Donald

Bill Duffell

Brett House

Jeremy and Wera Irvine

Cat Kennedy

John Newbury

Sally Wainman

Portadown swimmers completed a 1 mile sponsored swim for Angel Wishes and Jack

ABOUT THE AUTHORS

Emma Pusill learned to swim, after a fashion, in Morpeth Baths. She was considerably less keen on cold water then than she is now, and her overriding memory of those swimming trips was a sense of relief at being back in the changing cubicle. She came to lido swimming via the sea, having overcome a fear of swimming in the sea in her early forties. She is yet to develop an entirely cordial relationship with jellyfish, and considers one of the many advantages of lidos to be an absence of wildlife. She moved to Portishead because of the lido there, and being part of that community, as well as the wider lido community, has enriched her life immeasurably, as has her friendship with Janet – not least as it provides an opportunity to talk about lidos for literally hours without anybody rolling their eyes and looking bored. Emma is delighted to play a part in getting this book into the bags of swimmers everywhere, which is where it belongs.

Janet Wilkinson learned to swim in the entirely landlocked Leeds International Pool and developed her love of the pool at the coastal Derby Baths in Blackpool, neither of which exist any more. As a child her heart would leap at the idea that wherever her family was going on their UK holiday *might* have a swimming pool, and many, many hours were spent in indoor and outdoor pools alike, from Kent to the Clyde. Becoming a regular pre-9 a.m. swimmer at Parliament Hill Lido in the 1990s cemented her love of swimming outside and she's been on a quest to introduce others to their local open-air pools ever since. Meeting fellow lido-loving lunatic Emma has been one of the best things that has happened to her. Writing this long-dreamed-about book is something she'll always be grateful for the opportunity to pursue.

INDEX

SUPPORTERS

Unbound is the world's first crowdfunding publisher, established in 2011.

We believe that wonderful things can happen when you clear a path for people who share a passion. That's why we've built a platform that brings together readers and authors to crowdfund books they believe in – and give fresh ideas that don't fit the traditional mould the chance they deserve.

This book is in your hands because readers made it possible. Everyone who pledged their support is listed below. Join them by visiting unbound.com and supporting a book today.

@vicksvapourub/@StrandLido
Laura Adams
Michael Alexander
Erlend Alstad
Rachel Amner
Claudia Amos
Kathy Andrews
Carl Ape
Sarah Arnett
Chris Ash
Victoria Ashton
Martin Atkin
Tim Atkinson
Sue Bainborough
Alison Baker
Patricia Baker
Lisa Balderstone
Mary Baldwin
Helen Ball
Louise Barber
Jane Barnacle
Rosie Barnfield
Kim Barr
Pam Barrett
Sally Bartlett
Rebecca Bauer
Holly Baum
Beccles Lido
Ken Beedle
Louisa Bell
Sally Bell
Vicky Bellamy
Julia Bellis
Catherine Bellsham-Revell
Jane Bellworthy
Katy Bennett-Richards
Jon Beresford
Michelle Bird
Cathryn Bishop
Penny Blackburn
Janet Blair
John Blake
Jo Botham
Sarah Bower
Judith Bowler
Holly Bowman
Stee Boxer
Caroline Boyle
Dianne Brabham
Carol Bracken
Philip Bradby
Judith Bradford-Knox
Libby Bradshaw
Angela Bradshaw-Clifford
Kev Brady
Victoria Bramley
Uta Bräuer
Emma Brealey
Catherine Breslin
Viki Brice
Jean Briggs
Karen Brine
Caroline Broad
Brockwell Lido Users (BLU)
Brockwell Swimmers
Natasha Broke
Barb Brown
Colin Brown
Debbie Brown
Wilfred Edwin Brown
Jane Brown – In memory of Lynne Roper
Margaret Bruce
Dawn Brunning
Cathy Bryant
Isabel Bryony
A BS
Caroline Bullock
Anthony Bunge
Andrea Burden
Pat Burgess
Angie Butler
Kate C-p
Kerstin Cable

Jo Calam
Clare Calder
Robbie Campbell
Rebecca Campbell Wilson
Georgina Cape
Sally Capewell
Stephen Carleysmith
Alan Carpenter
Maria Carradice
Paul Cartwright
Maureen Casey
Lesley Chapman
Clare Charles
Paula Cherriman
Iona Chorley
David Clark
Neil Clasper
Ian Clewlow
Jeanine Clifford
Pam Cohen
Tiffany Coles
Laura Collett
Luke Collins
Emily Cook
Paul Stephen Coombes
Joyce Cooper
Barry Cooper & Maggie Pickering
Kath Coppin
Jane Core
Persis Cornet
Sue Coryndon
Nicola Court
Ian Coutts
Jane Cowling
Rachel Coyle
John Crawford
Karen Creavin
Julie Cribb
Andrea Crowe
Shaun Crowley
Julia Croyden
Suzanna Cruickshank
Matthew Cunio
Mark Currie
Nicholas Cutler
Luisa D'Lima
Annette Daly
Matthew Davenport
Ben Davies
Cheryl Davies
Cressida Davies
Jo Davies
Johanna Davies
Helen De Meyer
Mary Enna de Soissons
Chris Dean
Laurel Dean
Lucy Dearlove
Julie Dell
Emma Dixon
Marie Donnelly
Louise Doughty
Rosie Dowen
Cressida Downing
Kirstie Drummond Papworth
Charlotte Duff
Annette Duffell
Claire Duffell
Jeanette Duffell
Jeff Duffell
Katie Duffell
Bill Duffell Educational Fund
Laura Ellen Dunford
Christopher Durai-Bates
Peter Dwyer
Judith Dyer
Bryn Dymott
Charlie Eastabrook
Kathryn Eastman
Peter Edey
Hannah Edward
Juliet Edwards
Rebecca Edwards
Jenny Elberg
Libby Eley
Annalise Elliott
Susanna Eriksson-Lee
Glenys Evans
Sue Everard
Lynne Everson
Carlos Ezcurra
Nancy Farmer
Lucy Farrant
Charlotte Featherstone
Katy Ferguson
Steven Fewster
Fi & Al
Susan Fielding
Jon Finley
Moore Flannery
Kris Fleitz
Harriet Fletcher
Rachel Fletcher
John-Paul Flintoff
Simon Flood
Pat Flury
Ella Foote
DJ Fox
Alison Fox Hay
Julie Freeman
Sarah Freeman
John Frewin
Friends of Droitwich Spa Lido
Victoria Gaiger
Ceri Gallivan
Frances Gapper
Kathryn Garner
Dirk Gewert
Christine Gibbons
Rachel Gibson
Ana Gillespie
Marion Gillet
Fiona Gilmour
Sally Goble
Steven Goodchild
Baa Goodwin

Paul Goodwin
John Gourlay
Beverley Graham-Older
Bronwen Gray
Duncan Gray
Ros Gray
Sue Gray
Angela Green
Mel Greer-Walker
Jill Gregory
Chris Gribble
Sian Griffith
Lorna Guinness
Helen Hadley
Ann Hailwood
Mark Hailwood
Richard Haines
Andrew Haldane
Amanda Hall
Emma Hall
Clare Hall-Craggs
Tors Hamilton
Caro Hamilton McAdam
Paul Handley
John Hardaker
Neil Hardy
David Harley
Lisa Harrison
Justine Harvey
Alison Harvie
Amanda Harwood
Ruth Haynes
Sally Hebeler
Helen and Daniel
Alexandra Heminsley
Jane Hennessy
Alison Hepworth
Liz Hibbett
Helen Highley
Dan Hill
Wendy Hills
Philip Hirst
Historic Pools of Britain
Bob Holman
Steph Hope
Fiona Hopkins
Jacqueline Horne
Brett House
Liz Houston
Jen Howard
Peter Howarth
Lindsey Huchrak
Celia Hughes
Judi Hughes
Natalie Hughes
Rebecca Hughes
Anna Hull
Marion Hume
Karen Hunt
Beccy Huntley
Jeremy Irvine
Kate Isherwood
Wendy Ives
Polly Jaffé
Emma James
Simon James
Sophie Janacek
Branwen Jeffreys
Charles Jenkins
Jo & Liv and Jack the dog
Mark Johansen
Deborah Johns
Amanda Jones
Katy Jones
Libby Jones
Lucie Jones
Annika Joy
Rachel Judson
Debbie Kaye
Dee Keane
Desi Kearney
Hilary Kemp
Ellen Kemper
Cat Kennedy
Robert Kenney
Erika Kennington
Simon Kerslake
Ingrid Kibble
Dan Kieran
Mark Kilburn
For Jane Kilpatrick
KinaMara Swimwear
Charlotte King
Jackie King
Kathryn King
Fiona Kingston
Katie Kingwell
Hannah Knowles
Nicki Knox
Jenny Landreth
Ann Lanigan
Annabel Lavers
Joanne Lawson-Chilcott
Jack Layton
Pip Le Sage
Alfred Lea
Adam Leadbetter
Rosemary Leeke
Adam Legge
Tim Legge
Chloe Leila
Sydney Levinson
Emma Lewis
Ju Lewis
Helen Liddle
Mark Ling
Tamasin Little
Steve Lodge
Sam Long
Sophie Lovett
Lucy Luke
Helen Luker
Katy Lynch
Allan Macfadyen
Ian Macklin
Calum Maclean

Rachel MacLehose
Lala Mahakama
Hilary Maj
Catherine Makin
Dee Mammone
Simon Markall
Sharon Marks
Krishna Maroo
Clare Marshall
Howard Marshall
Dave Martin
Wueenie Martin
John Peter Maughan
Rhonda Mawer
Laura McDermott
Margaret McDonnell
Shawn McGuire
Karen McMahon
Rory McPherson
Sally-anne McWilliam
Tracy Mends
Susie Mesure
Jane Middleton
Julie Middleton
Amarylis Midgley
Keith Midgley
Phillipa Mills
Andrew Mimmack
LJ Minestrone
John Mitchinson
Sandra Moran
Michael Mordue
Moretonhampstead Swimming Pool Trust
Dom Morris
Beverley Mountford
Catherine Muirden
Bede Mullen
Annie Mulroy
Cressida Jane Murray
Sean Murray
Tim and Linda Murray
Jane Myburgh
Zoe Mylchreest
Bick Nalsdon
Carlo Navato
Clare Nestor
John Newbury
Hazel Nicholson
Billy Nomates
Mr November
Richard Nuell
Lisa Aqua Nut
Oonagh O'Brien
Kenneth O'Connor
Kevin and Rosalind O'Connor
Rebekah O'Sullivan
Elena Oliva
David Oliver
Robin Oliver
Judy and Pete Orme
Jess Orr
Libby Page
Sal Page
Wendy Pajak
Lotie Parker
Simon Parkin
Lisa Paton
Ashly Payne
Faye Peachey
Laura Peacock
Tim Peacock
Paula Pearson
Jeremy Pender
Cath Pendleton
Yolanda Perez-Shulman
Jennifer Peters
Wendy Petersen
Andrei Petrov
Andrew & Sue Phlido
Sophie Pierce
Jeremy Piggott
Gillian Pitman
Miss Plaistrust
Rachel Playforth
Sam Plum
Julie Pole
Justin Pollard
Chagford Pool
Sarah Poppy
Portadown ASC
Jason Potts
Alex Poulter
Carol Price
Alastair Pride
Ben Pridgeon
Karyn Probert
Julie Procter
Sophie Pusill
Imogen Radford
Susan Ramsden
Amanda Read
Rob Read
Fi Redpath
Kate Rew
Clare Reynolds
Alec Richardson
Susanna Riviere
Lucy Ellen Rix
Kate & Steve Robarts
David & Maretta Robinson
Freya Rodger
Scott Rodger
Liz Roe
Margaret Roe
Chris Romer-Lee, Studio Octopi & Thames Baths CIC
Lucy Roper
Tom Roper
Isobel Rorison
Amelia Ross
Elizabeth Ross
Caroline Rouse-Mighall
Clare Ruby
Penny Rushton
Helena Russell

Annie Salmon
Simon Sargeant
Helen Sargent
Justin Scarborough
Keith Scarborough
Julie Scherczer
Beverley Scholes
Matthew Scott
Sue Scott
Joseph Seliga
Gail Shackley
Tanya Shadrick
Tom Shakhli
Jay Sharp
Leonie Sharp
Laura Sharpe
Jim Sheeran
Paul Simons
Davy Simpson
Elizabeth Simpson
Kate Simpson
Ben Smith
Gillian Smith
Moira Smith
Paul Smith
Pauline Smith
Vicky Smith
Louise Snow
Carolyn Soakell
Rebecca Spencer
Ralph Sperring
Nathan Spilsted
Bronwen Stainsby
Joe Stanhope
Claire Stanyer
Jos Steinmann
Kathy Stevenson
Ruth Stoker
Amanda Stone
Simon Strickfuss
Carrie Sykes
Gila Tabrizi
Angie Tanner
Claire Taylor
Debbie Taylor
Nancy Taylor
Roger Taylor
Barbara Thatcher
David Thelwall
Sarah Thelwall
Sarah Thew
Ali Thompson
Diana Thompson
Gregory Thompson
Jane Thomson
Sally Tillett
Dominic Tinley
Margaret Tongue
Dougie Tri'gon
Amie Tridgell
Abby Troke
Mark Tucker
Martin Upham
Gerrie van Noord
Fiona Veacock
Kata Vizi
Hazel Vosper
Jenny Wade
Kate Wadee
Sally Wainman
Sally Walden
Michelle Walker
Jill Ward
Miranda Ward
Jane Warland
Julie Warren
Samantha Watkins
Verity Westgate
Sara Wex
Sarah Wheater
Matthew Whicher
Miranda Whiting
Ali Wigg
Hilary Wigg
Fiona Wiggins
Edward Wild
Christine Wilkinson
Alex Willatt
Beth Williams
Dawn Williams
Evan Williams
Rachel Williams
Duncan Wilson
Julie Wilson
Lawrence Wilson
Rich Wilson
Sally Wood
Sue Wood
Peter Woods
Liz Woolley
Diana Wray
Amy Wright
Gill Wright
Jackie Wright
Alexandra Wyatt
Mary Yardley
Hugh Young
James Young
Jonathan Young